MW00476105

Unraveling *the* Mysteries of Faith

GEORGE PANTAGES

George Pantages Ministries

Copyright © 2010 by George Pantages

Unraveling the Mysteries of Faith
by George Pantages

Printed in the United States of America
ISBN 978-0-9827695-1-5

All rights reserved solely by the author. The author guarantees all contents are original and do not infringe upon the legal rights of any other person or work. No part of this book may be reproduced in any form without the permission of the author. The views expressed in this book are not necessarily those of the publisher.

Unless stated otherwise, all Scripture references come from the NKJV translation of the Bible, copyright © 2006 Thomas Nelson.

KJV. Copyright © 2006 by Thomas Nelson.

New King James Version. Copyright © 1982 by Thomas Nelson, Inc. used by permission. All rights reserved.

George Pantages Ministries

George Pantages
Cell 512 785-6324
geopanjr@yahoo.com
Georgepantages.com

TABLE OF CONTENTS

Chapter 1
A DIFFERENT KIND OF SPIRIT................................ 11

Chapter 2
ACCORDING TO YOUR FAITH........................... 25

Chapter 3
BECOMING CHILDLIKE................................ 39

Chapter 4
WHERE IS YOUR FAITH?................................ 55

Chapter 5
IT'S JUST TOO HARD................................ 69

Chapter 6
WANTED: DEAD, NOT ALIVE................................ 83

Chapter 7
SENT BY GOD................................ 95

Chapter 8
PARADOXES................................ 109

Chapter 9
WHEN THE BOWL IS FULL................................ 121

Chapter 10
BEING SET UP FOR GREATNESS........... 137

DEDICATION

This book is dedicated to my lovely wife, Maria. The Lord brought her into my life at a time that it was in shambles. He has used her in the restoration process in a way that I never thought possible. I knew that picking up the pieces to my shattered life would be an all encompassing task, taking an exorbitant amount of time, exerting a ton of energy, and employing all the patience that I could muster. I wasn't too confident that I had the resolve to complete this assignment because the *Evil Day* had taken most of it away. Then this quiet, reserved, soft-spoken woman not only swept me off my feet, but was able to lead me to a place of normalcy in God with her patience and dry wit. I am laughing again without reservation and there is a constant smile on my face. I am at peace with myself and it has released me to be greater in God than I have ever been. The Scripture in Ephesians 3: 20 says that God...*is able to do exceeding abundantly above all that we ask or think.* Never in my wildest imaginations did I believe that God would bless me with such a wonderful woman as this. The Lord truly is a man of His word. I love you, *Cuqui,* with all my heart.

APPRECIATION

I would like to take the time to appreciate the following people for their contribution in publishing this book:

Michelle Levigne- English Editor

Jeser Garcia- Spanish Translator

Karen Contreras- Book Cover Design and Typesetting

Your professionalism and expertise rang true throughout the entire process, making my writing a whole lot better than it really is.

There were two church congregations both in the Houston area that helped sponsor this project and I would like to recognize the people that were generous in their giving.

Gold Donors ($1000)
Edwin & Yesenia Cerna
Santiago & Maricruz Torres

Silver Donors ($100)
Albert Garcia
Abel Cortez
Albert Salazar
Pastor Alfred Torres
Bilhan Fuentes
Carlos Medrano
Pastor Daniel Gordon
Esmeralda & Gabriel Delgadillo
Horacio Salazar
Iris Yamilet Gomez
Irma Zoloya
Israel & Maria Ramos
Jorge A. Lazo
Jorge & Melissa Salmeron
Jose & Raquel Cruz
Jose M. Martinez
Julio Cesar Samos Jr.
Margarita Alvarez
Maribel Umanzor
Romel & Beatriz Khan
Rosa Lovatos
Rose M. Reyes
Rosendo & Graciela Rosas
Ruben Montano
Yissell Martinez
Zully J. Millan

INTRODUCTION

Everyone loves a mystery, which is why mystery movies and books alike are such a big hit amongst their followers. Trying to figure out the plot and the various clues along the way before anyone else does lends us to give our full attention to every detail of the story. It is no wonder that movie studios and book publishing companies go out of their way to make sure that when their product is released no one has a clue as to how it will end. Millions and millions of dollars are then spent with the purpose of unraveling these mysteries right before their eyes.

Sadly to say, when the mysteries of the Christian life come our way, we do not venture out with the same vigor to solve them. Although it would appear that the Christian's life imitates art, with unsolvable mysteries, this was never the Lord's intention for the body of Christ. The paradoxes we face as Christians were not designed to confuse or frustrate us to no end, but rather to use as stepping stones to get to a place where we could unleash our faith. These paradoxes, though unexplainable, without rhyme or reason, are the building blocks God uses to help us formulate a life of faith. We must be willing to throw logic and reasoning to the wind so it will speed up the process of allowing God full control of our lives.

If we can get to that point, then we will be able to render null and void the erroneous lessons of faith that have been passed down to us from prior generations, right the wrong, and move into a realm of faith that will be pleasing to God.

LORD, MAY THE UNRAVELING BEGIN!!!

Chapter 1
A DIFFERENT KIND OF SPIRIT

"But my servant Caleb, because he has had a different spirit and has followed Me fully, I will bring into the land which he entered, and his descendants shall take possession of it.
(Num 14:24, (NASB)

As I was returning from lunch one day, a coworker of mine approached me in the parking lot with a request. She asked me if I would mind speaking to a friend of hers who congregated in her local church. It appeared that this young lady no longer wanted to continue going to church, and my coworker was somewhat puzzled as to why. I reluctantly said yes, and we made our way up to the conference room. I was hesitant because when I'm not behind a pulpit ministering, I am very insecure and fearful. Counseling a young lady who I did not know and had never seen before really took me out of my comfort zone. I began asking God for a word of knowledge to help me understand the direction that He wanted me to go. From past experience, I knew that I would only receive a portion of what I was going to say, and that always made me nervous. Knowing that revelation is always progressive still doesn't ease the butterflies that I feel when I am chosen to be God's mouthpiece.

I felt the tension in the room and sensed the young lady really didn't want to hear what I was about to say. She had already made up her mind that going to church and serving God was not an option. Then revelation came.

I told her that the reason she no longer wanted to go to that particular church was that although her Pastor was bilingual, speaking both Spanish and English, he preferred to go with his strength, which was Spanish. Of course her preference was English, and she really wasn't getting anything out of the sermons and lessons he gave. As soon as those words came out of my mouth, her body language completely changed. Her facial expressions clearly said, *How in the world did you know that? I had never mentioned that to anyone.* Knowing that I had broken the ice, I continued to seek God for more revelation.

What came next, I knew, was not only going to be difficult for me to say, but probably even more so for her to hear. I began to feel the presence of the Lord so strongly that it appeared as if He completely took over this conversation. Feeling His ever-loving touch and warmth, with tears welling up in my eyes, I said, "You are very, very angry with God right now because you felt that He did not protect you when your daddy began to sexually abuse you. You felt that if God was such a loving God, He would have never permitted this nightmare to ever happen to you. How can God say that He loves me when it happened over and over and over again? Where was He when I needed Him most? And to make matters worse, he has already started on my younger sisters as well."

By this time, the tears streamed uncontrollably down her cheeks, and my coworker was equally startled by the words that she had just heard. Now that this ugly secret was out in the open, and God had revealed to a stranger her most intimate thoughts and fears, she was ready to open up her heart. Her countenance completely changed, and I began to minister to her in a way that allowed the Spirit of God to not only comfort her at the moment, but give her hope for the future as well. I still remember the bewildered look on her face as she left the conference room that day. She kept asking my coworker, "How did he know, how did he know all about me?"

As I began to ponder myself what had actually happened just moments before, I realized that a different kind of Spirit had moved upon me.

Now that I have caught your attention, some of you are probably asking, "What in the world is a different kind of Spirit, and how can I get one?" Right off the bat let me say this. For those of you who are looking for something above and beyond the Spirit of God that you have already received, forget it. When you were baptized in His Spirit, you received all of the power of God that you will ever need to be successful in Him. This will be covered a little bit more deeply later in the book. But for argument's sake, understand this. A different kind of Spirit is not another Spirit apart from the Holy Spirit of God, although it would appear to be so. A different kind of Spirit is that same Holy Ghost that lived inside of Jesus Christ as He walked on this earth. It is a Spirit that is alive, vibrant, obedient, and so in tune with His Spirit that it wrecks mayhem, making the devil's life miserable.

CALEB's DIFFERENT KIND OF SPIRIT

One day, Moses picked 12 men to go out and spy the Promised Land, with Joshua and Caleb being two of them. Their assignment that day was to go out and find out where everything was strategically positioned. They were to come back with a report that would identify all of the blessings that God had promised the children of Israel. In what started out as an easy assignment, taking an inventory of all that would eventually be theirs, 10 spies were distracted by the giants, the walled cities, and all the weapons of destruction that the Canaanites possessed. Instead of returning with a positive report as instructed, their fear overwhelmed them and they returned with a negative opinion instead.

A person with a different kind of Spirit is not blind to what everyone else is looking at. Neither does he necessarily see things that no one else sees.

What he does do is this: He looks at situations that others are looking at, but with the eyes of God. What has been revealed and promised to him by God are sufficient to stand on when circumstances and situations say differently. I can imagine how livid they were when they heard the others complain that the land was too great to conquer. God had already promised them the victory; all they had to do was go in and take it. Did they honestly believe that God did not know that there were giants in the land? Was He unaware that they were great warriors as well? Did He miss the boat when He believed that the Israelites could take the walled cities? Would it take some doing? Yes! Were they out of their league? Absolutely not! Whatever they were not able to accomplish on their own strength, God would make up the difference with the power of His Spirit. They just needed to believe God for His word. For this, their thoughts would have to change.

A person with a different kind of Spirit will not only see things differently, but his thought patterns will also be different. His obedience to God is such that he will do things that he does not understand. I am pretty sure that when Caleb began to write down all that he saw, there was the temptation to write down the same negative stuff that the rest of the spies saw. But he understood that his assignment only included him returning with a report and not his own opinion. His ability to stay focused helped him to come back with a report that God was looking for. It also protected him from returning negative, pessimistic, and defeated. A different kind of Spirit will do that. It will reveal the mysteries of God. Mysteries that must be held onto, even when the rest of the world thinks you're crazy. Although Caleb's report was positive, optimistic, and encouraging, it was completely rejected by the rest. They just couldn't understand his different kind of Spirit.

STANDING AGAINST THE MAJORITY

A willingness to stand against the majority must be accepted if a different kind of Spirit is going to flow through you freely. Why? Because the majority rarely understands a person used by God in this fashion. They are too odd, strange, bizarre, and out of the ordinary to be accepted by most. But this is how the Apostle Paul states it in 1Corinthians 2:14:

> *But the natural man does not receive the things of the Spirit of God, for they are foolishness to him; nor can he know them, because they are spiritually discerned.*

15

Most Christian people are offended by the fact that they are being lumped into the same group as people who do not know God, i.e., natural man. But the fact of the matter is this: any Christian who does not follow the guidelines set out by the Lord in His word, to continue growing in His Spirit, does fall back into his old nature. There are too many Christians in the world today who, although Spirit-filled, are not really Spirit-led. That is why the reactions to the visionaries and dreamers of this age are exactly the way Joshua and Caleb were greeted by the children of Israel, with hatred and disgust. The Israelites were so incensed by the report given by these two men that they were already picking up stones to kill them.

I remember a situation that I was highly criticized for some years back. A different kind of Spirit came over me and did something that many considered out of order. I was ministering in a somewhat large congregation, and those who had come to the altar that day were many. In those days, I would take all comers one by one and, depending on the crowd, would take up a sufficient amount of time. I would begin at one end of the altar, slowly making my way to the other side, praying that there would be enough time to minister to everyone who had come.

After several minutes at the altar, a young lady about 12 years old came up to me and gently tapped me on the shoulder. She had been stricken with Down syndrome and had the mentality of a five-year-old.

She said, "Sir, do you see that tall thin lady on the other side of the altar?"

I turned around located her mom and said, "Yes."

She continued, "Do you think you can make your way down to where she's at right now? She's really in a lot of pain and I know God can heal her."

"Sure," I said. "Just give me five minutes and I'll be right there, okay?"

With a nod, she ran back to where Mama was, believing that in a few moments God was going to heal her. About two minutes later, she ran back to where I was at and, a bit more agitated, tapped me on the shoulder a little bit harder. "Sir, didn't you hear me? My mom is on the other side and she needs your help right now, okay?"

I responded, "I'm sorry, young lady, just give me a couple more minutes and for sure I'll be there, okay?

With another nod of approval, she ran back to where Mama was, and waited for me. One minute later, she scampered back where I was and began shaking me insistently, shouting, "Sir, didn't you hear me? My mom is over there and she needs your help."

At this time, I received a different kind of Spirit and said this: "I tell you what. Go back to your mom and stand behind her. Put your hands on her shoulders and say this: *"In the name of Jesus, be healed, and pain be gone."*

Excited that God was finally going to heal her mom, she ran back to where Mama was and did exactly as she was told. Immediately, the stiff neck that restricted any kind of movement was loosened completely. Her mom began to move it back and forth without any pain whatsoever. The two of them got real happy, and rightfully so. But that wasn't the only reaction when this woman was healed. According to a lot of folks, I was out of order, sending a young lady who was not an ordained minister to do that kind of job in the church. Much like the reaction that Jesus received when He would heal people on the Sabbath, I was chastised because things were not done that way in that particular church.

I made sure that I did not disobey any rules of that organization, I just found a loophole. The rules state that only an ordained minister can lay hands on the heads of those who need healing. I had the young lady lay hands on her mama's shoulders, knowing that I was within the limits of Scripture,

> *And these signs will follow those who believe:......they will lay hands on the sick, and they will recover."*
>
> (Mark 16:17-18)

To this day, it still amazes me how people can discount the miraculous things that God is doing, just because it does not fit into the mold that they are accustomed to.

AGE IS NOT A FACTOR

This leads us to another factor that does not hinder a person who has received a different kind of Spirit. Age. Age and experience, or the lack thereof, seems to be the common thread of excuse for those who never fall into the will of God. Physically, the elderly cannot contribute just because their bodies will not let them. Married folk throw their hat into the arena by saying that they are just too busy, trying to establish themselves to give their families a better life. Then there are the young people, very astute in avoiding their responsibilities. They bring to the table the best excuse, at least in their eyes, that although they are very willing to enter into the will of God; in truth it is impossible because they just don't know how. All the while, people are dying each day without Christ, and the Church continues to search for somebody who will step up to the plate.

There is one thing for sure: Caleb would have none of this. When it was time to distribute the inheritance of the Promised Land, look at what Caleb asked for. At the age of 85, he asked Joshua to give him the part of the land infested with giants. He was fearless in thinking that even at this age; these giants were no match for God's people.

> *As yet I am as strong this day as on the day that Moses sent me; just as my strength was then, so now is my strength for war, both for going out and for coming in. Now therefore, give me this mountain of which the LORD spoke in that day; for you heard in that day how the Anakim were there, and that the cities were great and fortified. It may be that the LORD will be with me, and I shall be able to drive them out as the LORD said."*
>
> (Josh 14:11-12)

Was this just an old man, past his prime, trying to impress the leader of Israel? I am pretty sure he understood that physically, he wasn't the same man that Moses sent originally to spy out the land. Nevertheless, the one thing that he knew he had going for him was this: God was on his side, and His power never changes. Without a shadow of a doubt, whatever was needed to get the job done, somehow or another God would provide. Although the circumstances had changed drastically since Moses had given him the promise of his inheritance,

Caleb was willing to stand on that promise, believing that God would make good on it no matter how long it would take for them to get there.

One Sunday before the morning service, a member of a particular church walked into the Pastor's office. He had just left the hospital, shaken by the news given to him by the doctors. They woefully admitted that whatever was wrong with his wife at that time, which they could not figure out, it was rapidly killing her. He pleaded with the Pastor to please pray for her, knowing that only God would be able to heal her. As the Pastor approached the pulpit that morning, he received a different kind of Spirit.

He mentioned to the congregation the need that morning, and then made this statement. "I'm not really sure why I'm about to say this, but I believe that it's from God. If there is anyone here who can recite from memory St. John chapter 15, God will send an angel of healing to that hospital room right now and heal our sister." As he gazed over the entire congregation, his eyes first glanced over to the adult section. Out of embarrassment, most of the adults had hung their heads, hoping that the Pastor would not call on them. As he continued to search out into the congregation, his eyes then fell upon the young people's group. Their reaction was even more pronounced. Some were bent over completely; others appeared to be making their way under the pew.

But there in the back of this church of about 400 was a little girl, jumping up and down saying, "Pastor, Pastor, I know it, choose me. Really Pastor, I really do know it, choose me." Of course, all of the people around her tried to calm her down, believing that she had misunderstood the Pastor's request. But she was insistent that she could help out in this situation, if only the Pastor would call her up to the front. At long last, the Pastor looked over to this little jumping bean and asked her to come to the platform. When she arrived, the Pastor wanted to know how was it that she happened to know this portion of Scripture. She said, "My mama home schools me, and every month I have a portion of Scripture to memorize. This month I had to memorize all of John 15 and I want to be used by God today." She boldly stood before the congregation and began to recite this chapter that has 27 verses. After reciting about five verses, the Spirit of the Lord entered into the back of the sanctuary.

After about 10 verses, the Spirit became more pronounced as it began to move through the people. After 15 verses, the Spirit had now reached about half of the congregation and many began to weep. When she had finished reciting 20 verses, it had reached the entire congregation. For the last seven verses, people could no longer control the glory that had fallen upon them and collectively began to worship openly. At the end of her reciting, the Pastor stood before the congregation, commanding an angel of healing to find its way to that hospital room. It was at that moment that that woman felt a touch of God and was healed.

Thousands of years have passed since the initial outpouring of the Holy Ghost on the day of Pentecost. We are slowly inching our way to understanding its use and purpose in our lives, yet many times we get distracted. I don't think that we purposely mean to hoard all of the blessings to ourselves, however, what God has made available to everyone in this world usually ends up in our hands only. To make matters worse, sometimes we don't even make it accessible to many in the church.

There are far too many Christians today who wander aimlessly, without a clue as to what the will of God is in their lives. They search and they search, not knowing where to go, what to do, or how to get their answers. They believe that their God is an unreachable kind of God. And if that be true, what's the use of looking for answers in the first place? If only there were more people around today with a different kind of Spirit. Ones who are sensitive to the needs of others and are not afraid to venture out into the unknown, helping those who are in despair.

This is not only needed desperately in the church, but in the lost world as well. It is time to step out of the four walls and reach the masses of unsaved people with a different kind of Spirit.

AN UNEXPECTED REQUEST

I was in my office one day, fasting, when about lunchtime I heard the voice of the Lord. Or at least I thought it was the voice of the Lord. He said, "I would like you to end your fast now." Without any kind of explanation, I was somewhat bewildered by His request. My first impression was this: *That's not the voice of God that I'm hearing, that's the devil. God is usually asking me for more of my time not less. This has to be a trick from the enemy.*

As I continued to ponder on what I had just heard, the Lord spoke to me again. "No, no, it's really me. Go ahead and end your fast, it's okay with me." I felt really uneasy about it, but I was so hungry that I hurried up to my favorite restaurant before He could change His mind. I wasn't feeling too guilty, because I had been reading a really good book on prayer and I thought if anything, reading the book would be my spiritual exercise for the day. As I walked into the restaurant, it was completely full. There wasn't enough time to wait for an open table, and I pondered what to do next.

The Lord spoke to me again and said, "Go around the corner and eat there." As I went outside of the restaurant and looked in the direction where God was sending me, I thought that the Lord was getting back at me for ending my fast prematurely. Lo and behold, in front of me stood a McDonald's restaurant. "Oh well," I said. "At least I have a good book that I am going to be reading and that will make up for the food I am about to eat." I hurriedly sat down, knowing that I was running out of time, when I received a different kind of Spirit.

In front of me in the next booth sat a young married lady with a far away look in her eyes. Her two adorable daughters, about the ages of two and three, were running around with her not paying too much attention. When the Lord spoke to me, He said this: "Go to the next booth and minister to this young lady. I will tell you what to say when you get there."

I was completely terrified by this assignment because it was not only in public, but in a crowded place. As I got up and stood before her, the words were hard to come by. The few moments that I was there seemed to be like hours. She looked straight at me, and without a word her eyes were screaming at me, saying, *Well buddy, are you going to stand there all day looking at me, or do you have something to say?*

Finally, after what appeared to be an eternity, God gave me these words. "I know that you're feeling really bad right now because last night when your husband came home from work, he told you that the marriage was over. He found someone else to love and he had only come home that evening to pack his bags and say goodbye. It had caught you completely by surprise, and now as you have had time to think about it, you just don't know what to do." She did not react to my words one iota. There was no emotion, no tears, no nothing. I could feel my face getting red from embarrassment because I thought I had completely missed the boat.

I didn't know what to do, when God told me to ask her if it was okay for me to pray for her. It was then that the tears in her eyes began to well up. At long last, I knew I had struck a nerve. I laid my hands on her in the midst of the lunch hour rush, praying that God would not only console her, but would bring the peace that was so badly needed to help her go on. It wasn't a prayer for salvation or that God would baptize her with the Holy Ghost. It was a prayer that would speak to her greatest need at this time, which was her sanity. I quietly dismissed myself from her and I sat down once again to continue reading. A short while later, she gathered her belongings with her two babies, and for a moment stood in front of me without a word. As I looked into her crystal blue eyes, slowly the tears began to well up and fall. Finally, with lips trembling, she simply said, "Thank you," and left.

Needless to say, the call for a different kind of Spirit cannot be overstated. How we have used this most precious gift has left something to be desired. We have miserably fallen short of what God had intended it to be. But there still is a glimmer of hope, because according to our faith in God, God can still accomplish the impossible. That is the subject of our next chapter.

Chapter 2
ACCORDING TO YOUR FAITH

*When Jesus departed from there, two blind
men followed Him, crying out and saying, "Son
of David, have mercy on us!" And when He had
come into the house, the blind men came to
Him. And Jesus said to them, "Do you believe
that I am able to do this?" They said to Him,
"Yes, Lord." Then He touched their eyes,
saying, "According to your faith let it be to
you."*

(Matt 9:27-29)

Several years ago E.F. Hutton ran a commercial that
was very effective. There was a gathering of people who
were mingling and talking freely amongst themselves.
Because of the ongoing chitter chatter; no one was paying
attention to any particular conversation. All of a sudden
somebody utters, "According to E.F. Hutton..." and the
entire room stops to hear what this person is about to say.
According to their understanding, whatever E.F. Hutton
had to say was important enough to stop whatever they

were doing and get in on the scoop. It is amazing what can happen to a group of people when somebody with that kind of clout walks in. That person can just about hold that group hostage, for they are spellbound by his every word. That is exactly what happens when you release your faith. In the spirit world, everyone comes to attention. They wait with bated breath for their instructions so that you can make the earth as it is in Heaven.

THE FAITH OF TWO BLIND MEN

Sad to say, most Christians today don't come to grips with this truth. In their minds, that kind of power and authority is delegated to the elite in the kingdom. For them, the glorious benefits of Christianity don't start till they get to Heaven. Boy, have we truly been duped by the enemy on this one. Let's take a look at these two blind men we find in the book of Matthew, and see what kind of faith they had that allowed them to receive their miracle.

At first glance, how they are calling on the Master gives us a glimpse of the faith that they possess. The term *"Son of David"* was commonly used in those times to denote the coming Messiah. All of Israel knew the promise given to David that the Messiah would come from his seed, and this is exactly what the blind men were referring to when they made their call to Jesus. How could there be faith in a man they could not see? By hearing, of course! Does not faith come by hearing? It surely does, and the fame of this God man was running rampant in the streets of Israel for all to hear.

Their petition onto Him was simply, "Have mercy on us," which demonstrates more faith than meets the eye. Notice how they did not ask Jesus to heal them. They understood that the son of David, their Messiah, would be merciful (PS 72:12-13), and if the mercy that He would show them that day were to include the healing of their blinded eyes, so be it. But they were pleading for His mercy by faith.

They persisted to validate their faith by continuing to follow Him when He did not respond to their initial cries. Bill Johnson states in his book *Dreaming with God* that God doesn't hide blessings *from us* but rather *for us*. Things are hidden from the surface so that our hunger for them will take us to a deeper level of seeking, so that we might find them. Once we find ourselves in uncharted waters, we are encouraged to let the Spirit of God guide us into areas of revelation that are not normally found amongst most of His children.

That is what ultimately motivated these two blind men. No one else had their unique problem, so their desperate situation required a desperate measure. They continued to cry out by faith, and when Jesus left them outside as He walked into a house, they pursued Him without skipping a beat. Now that's faith.

Finally, the last show of faith comes when Jesus asks the ultimate question, *"Do you believe that I am able to do this?"* (vs.28). It would have been a total waste of effort if, at this point, they would not have verbally responded with a resounding yes.

Once your thoughts and beliefs of what God is going to do in your life become verbal, there's no holding back. God will honor your words and your faith, and the solution to your problem is nothing more than an afterthought. But it has to come out of your mouth. What actually happens when we do this is that we put God on the spot. Not that we are trying to force God to do something that He does not want to do.

27

We have done our part, and now it's time for Him to do His part. The ball now lies in His court, and because He has to be true to His word, the rest is a slam dunk. When the blind men had an opportunity to respond, their immediate response of, "Yea Lord," without hesitation, brought the miracle they so desperately sought after. As soon as the words left their mouths, the answer was on its way. God always honors faith.

I believe now is a good time to ask some questions that bear asking: How do I obtain that kind of faith? How much experience is needed in order to see God move in such a marvelous fashion? Does God actually have that kind of time to show me the way? Let's see if I can answer those questions and more by observing the life of David.

DAVID'S RELENTLESS PURSUIT OF GOD

He was a highly skilled young man in the ways of the Spirit at such a tender age. Why? Because he learned at the outset that spending time in the presence of God would be the key to knowing God. It would not be uncommon for him to meditate on God while he cared for his father's sheep. Not so much that he was negligent in his responsibilities for that stage in time. He used his time wisely, and when he found a lull in his work, he spent it in the presence of God.

> *In Your presence is fullness of joy; At Your right hand are pleasures forevermore.*
>
> (Ps 16:11)

The more he entertained the Spirit of God in His presence, the fuller his life became. It made him a better shepherd, a better son, a better musician, a better songwriter. He became the best example of what a sold-out young man could do for God. With every moment spent worshiping and adoring His creator, there came the confidence and faith to believe that nothing was impossible for His God.

I remember a time in high school when, playing football, I had a similar faith, regarding playing the game of course. During the summertime, I would in reality live at my school. I would get there early in the morning and I would not leave until they closed the doors at night. I had two goals during that time. First, to become the best place kicker in Southern California, and second, to win a football scholarship to a Division I school in college. I was relentless in my pursuit of those goals. I decided that my social life was going to be kept to a bare minimum, meaning no girlfriends. I was going to spend the rest of my free time away from practice studying and hitting the books.

I remember spending so much time on our football field that I had kicked from every possible spot that I would be called on to kick a field goal. Day in and day out, it didn't matter what I was losing out on, my passion to be the best drove me incessantly.

When the season finally began, I felt like I could confidently kick a ball from any part of the field blindfolded and still be successful. That is how high my faith and confidence had risen.

What about the goals that I had set? Both of them were reached just as I had hoped. I set a kicking record that stood for 15 years, was named to the All Southern California football team (1st team), and won a football scholarship to the University of Southern California (USC).

The revelation and blessing to be gained by spending time in the presence of God far outweigh the losses that will be incurred. The secrets and the mysteries revealed will be mind-boggling. You will not only increase your faith, but it will be so much so that signs and wonders will become a normal occurrence in your everyday life. The time that David spent wooing God in prayer allowed him to unleash his faith, permitting such an enormous growth that it prepared him to continue climbing the ladder of success. His assignments in God became more varied in nature and in difficulty. When his father's flocks were bothered by a lion, he calmly took matters into his own hands and killed it. When a bear much bigger and stronger than the lion tried doing the same, it too was no match for this faith-filled shepherd boy. Now with David's faith growing by leaps and bounds, he encountered a Philistine giant that caused havoc in the camp of Israel. Although this target was much bigger, stronger, and much savvier in the art of war, in David's mind it didn't matter. His God only needed to be called upon to wipe out this harmless threat. With one swing of his sling, down goes Frazier (oops, I meant Goliath). As simplistic as it appears, increasing faith truly does come from hearing the voice of God while in His presence.

A MISUNDERSTOOD CONCEPT OF FAITH

Now, I would like to clear up something that has been misunderstood or at least has not been completely explained correctly for some time. There is a universally known Scripture about releasing our faith that causes more confusion than most. I would like to focus some time on it.

*So then faith comes by hearing, and hearing by
the word of God.*

(Rom 10:17)

We have been taught now for generations if that we
hear the written word of God by whatever means, it will
increase our faith. The fact of the matter is that it's both
true and false. The key to understanding the Scripture in
its entirety falls on the translation of the word, "word."
Most of the time "word" is translated as "logos," and
rightfully so. By definition, it translates as the written
Word of God. The problem that we find in Romans 10:17 is
that the Greek "word" used in this instance is "rhema."

Rhema is translated as the "saying" word of God. Now
then, there are times that the written Word can be rhema,
but rhema doesn't necessarily have to be written the word
of God. If we limit the definition of rhema to only the
written Word of God, then we forfeit the Spirit of God
speaking to us on a daily basis.

This is where most people miss it. In times of need, we
have been taught to open up the Bible, find a Scripture
that applies to our situation, and claim it by faith. Unless
the Lord has specifically guided you to that particular
Scripture and instructed you to live on it by faith, your
efforts are nothing more than hit-or-miss. I have seen so
many people use this method without success, that they
have hopelessly given up on stepping out by faith
completely.

JOSEPH'S RHEMA FROM GOD

On the other hand, whether the written Word of God
or the Spirit of the Lord have spoken to us through a
rhema, then our faith can be loosed to believe God,

regardless of the circumstances. If there ever was a man in the Bible who had to disregard all of the negative things that came to his life after a rhema, it was Joseph. Even as a lad, he was favored by his father. This show of affection only caused strife amongst his brothers, which came to a head when he shared a dream he had had. According to the dream and its interpretation, there would come a time in the near future when he, Joseph, would rule over all of them.

A rhema will always bring out the naysayers, including the devil. It is his job to mess up any and all promises of God that we have received, so expect the opposition to be greater. Little did Joseph know that the time of testing would be strung out for 13 years. In that time period, for all of the losses that he was expected to endure, the only thing that he had going for him was his dream. His life began its downward slide when his brothers sold him as a slave, and he ultimately landed in Egypt. It amazes me, the resolve that this young man demonstrated. Maybe he was too young and inexperienced to know that his dream had just died. Nevertheless, whatever his hand found to do, he did it with all his might, and was successful at that. Potipher detected this and immediately made him the overseer in his house. His boss's favor only brought more trouble when Potipher's wife falsely accused him of attempted rape. Although jail time was not part of the dream, he made the most out of a bad situation by continuing to minister. He found himself interpreting dreams of other prisoners but was forgotten until two years later. Can't a guy catch a lucky break? He didn't need one; he had a dream, a rhema from God that kept him believing when no one else would. At long last, he found himself in the presence of

Pharaoh with an opportunity of a lifetime.

All he had to do was interpret a dream that Pharaoh had, and it got him his get out of jail card. Thirteen years had now come and gone, and still there was no trace of bitterness or anger in the heart of this dreamer. The journey that brought his dream into reality had in truth taken on a life of its own with many potholes along the way. Needless to say, holding onto his dream got him through the worst of times. So much so that he never lost hope, and boldly proclaimed this to Pharaoh:

> *"It is not in me; God will give Pharaoh an answer of peace."*
>
> (Gen 41:16)

He never lost sight of where his ability came from, making sure that God would always receive the honor and the glory for any of his success.

As he interpreted Pharaoh's dream, his own dream in actuality began to unfold. In time, he ascended to second place in Pharaoh's kingdom, which gave him the jurisdiction over the area where his family lived. When they were forced to come to Egypt for food, Joseph had an opportunity for payback. As he dealt with them, making known his true identity, fear of retaliation gripped their hearts. Only a man who had a preview of the future, regardless of countless setbacks, could respond to them the way he did.

He was a man with a true rhema from God. Listen to his words:

> *But as for you, you meant evil against me; but God meant it for good, in order to bring it*

about as it is this day, to save many people alive.

(Gen 50:20)

For all of the nights spent in that dark and dreary jail cell, alone with his thoughts, with no one to confide in, he would continue to learn to fight according to his faith. It was his faith and his faith alone that God honored, to make an impossible dream a reality.

I would like to close out this chapter by sharing a testimony of something that happened in my life a few years ago. I believe it will speak to those without much experience in hearing and understanding the voice of God.

MY INITIAL ENCOUNTER WITH RHEMA

Back in the 80s, I received a phone call that would completely turn my life upside down. My cousin, Richard, was on the other line with bad news. I remember him asking me, "George, are you sitting down?" He continued sullenly saying, "What I am about to say is going to be hard to swallow, but the doctors have found tumors at the base of Tabitha's (his wife) brain and are inoperable." For a period of time now, Tabitha was experiencing seizures that were causing complications throughout her entire body. We had been praying, believing that God was going to heal her completely when I received this phone call. This new prognosis of her condition really affected me adversely. For days I walked around aimlessly, confused, dazed, and somewhat angry at God for allowing something like this to happen to one of the most precious and godly women I knew. Unbeknownst to me, God was

34

about to use the situation not only to restore her health, but also to increase my faith to levels that I never thought were possible.

God came to me one day with a request that made me furious. He was inviting me to begin a 21-day fast in Tabitha's behalf. It would be absolute in nature, meaning for this period of time I would only be drinking water. What had really incensed me was not so much the task at hand, but rather who was being asked to perform it. I was neither experienced nor competent to complete such a request. Conversely, at that point in time, my cousin Richard was light-years ahead of me in his use of faith. I knew without a shadow of a doubt that this job was right up Richard's alley, so then why was this enormous responsibility being placed on my shoulders?

Like a spoiled brat, I kicked and complained and cried before God, pleading with Him to release me from this assignment. Sadly on my part, His mind was made up, having complete confidence in his initial choice, me. With my attitude in the wrong place, horribly bad, I began my quest. After just a day, I hopelessly gave up; grumpily muttering to God that he had made a big mistake and it couldn't be done. He gently encouraged me to try again, and you don't know how much it took me to humble myself, but I did and started again. This time, I lasted for three days, with the end result being the same. I had broken the fast again before the appointed time. Now really feeling inept, facing God in prayer was going to be an unpleasant encounter. With kid gloves and much understanding, He once again admonished me to start anew. But this time, He included something to do while in prayer that made no sense at all. He proposed that every day in prayer, for half an hour, I was to extend both arms in front of me, opening and closing my hands, and repeating these words. SHRINK THE TUMORS IN JESUS' NAME!

At that time, I was attending a church that opened its doors at 4 a.m. for prayer. Knowing that hardly anybody would show up to pray at that ungodly hour, I made up my mind to pray when the doors opened. I wanted as few people as possible watching me go through my little routine, so that I could avoid total embarrassment. There is a saying that, "the third time is the charm." In my third attempt of fasting, that was genuinely a true statement. Each morning thereafter, I faithfully went to the church, going through my little practice, believing God for this miracle.

One of the greatest lessons I learned during this time of consecration was that in the interim, the presence of God was nowhere to be found. I had been under the assumption that if one was going to take the time to completely dedicate himself unto the Lord during that time, great visions and manifestations of God would be commonplace. To the contrary, my prayers were completely dry and listless. The voice of God was silent. The only motivation I had to complete this task was in the form of the memory of one of my best friends. She desperately needed my help, and I was going to do the best that I could to oblige.

The time of fasting had finally come to an end, and it had taken its toll. Physically I was drained, emotionally I was spent, and spiritually my only consolation that I could hang a hat on was the fact that I had obeyed the voice of God. There were no new levels of understanding or wisdom. There were no feelings of supremacy in any way. There were thoughts that continued to haunt me, questioning myself whether I had actually done this thing right. After a week of second-guessing I received a phone call from Richard. He said, "I just received the latest test results on Tabitha and there is something unexplainable that has happened. She is no longer in danger of dying. The doctors have told me that the tumors have shrunk and they don't know why." When I heard the word shrunk, I almost jumped up and started dancing. Finally I understood why God had asked of me what He did. He wanted to connect what I was doing in prayer to the miracle that He was doing in Tabitha. For all the times during the fast that I had questioned God, the end result was more spectacular than I could imagine. This brought a favorite Scripture to mind:

> *Now to Him who is able to do exceedingly abundantly above all that we ask or think, according to the power that works in us, to Him be glory in the church by Christ Jesus to all generations, forever and ever. Amen.*
> (Eph 3:20-21)

When the *power that works in us* is put into action according to our faith, He is not only willing, but able to bring blessings into our lives that we could not have possibly imagined. For me, for the first time in all my years serving the Lord, I was a major participant in watching God perform a miracle, helping me break through to another level of faith. For Tabitha and her family, it was an opportunity to be on the receiving end of a great miracle.

There will come times in your life in God when, in your eyes, He will make silly requests without explanation.

Our job is not to question or try to analyze. Our job is to take God at His word, put it into action and watch His hand move. If we can trust Him the way a child does, unreservedly, then according to our faith will it be done unto us. That is the focus of the next chapter.

Chapter 3
BECOMING CHILDLIKE

*And said, "Assuredly, I say to you, unless you
are converted and become as little children,
you will by no means enter the kingdom of
heaven.*

(Matt 18:3)

Becoming childlike in the kingdom of God does not
mean that we must become childish. The definition of
both words start out the same, i.e., relating to a child;
nevertheless their differences are like night and day.
When one is being childish, it talks to the immaturity and
lack of poise in childhood. Being childlike, on the other
hand, moves more towards the innocence or trust found in
a child. Because of its negative connotation, childhood is
viewed as a necessary evil. There is always a great hurry
to grow up, especially in the things of the Lord, because
we don't want to be considered immature. Wisdom does
not necessarily come automatically with age, it must be
sought out. It is then somewhat childish to believe that
because you have reached that stage of adulthood,

wisdom is waiting for you as you arrive.

As we examine the words of Jesus written to us in the book of Matthew, we find that His view of childhood is completely different. As He sits a little one on His lap, He warns those within earshot that unless they are converted and become as this child, chances of making Heaven are impossible. What could have prompted such an outlandish statement? Perhaps it was advance warning that serving Him in the kingdom of God would be an experience like none other. Like a child, he would be able to receive his orders and complete them, without understanding them completely. Like a child, he could easily forgive and forget when his heart had been broken. Finally, like a child, his love for God would be pure and unconditional.

The key to this new mindset would be the ability to be converted. Change does not come easy for most of us, but with a pledge of loyalty and single-mindedness, anything is possible. The sooner we humble ourselves to allow God to have complete control in our lives, the sooner we will take on the childlike characteristics that He is looking for, so that someday we can make Heaven our home. I have discovered three characteristics in childhood that we as adults have pretty much left behind. Let's study these childlike characteristics one by one.

LEARNING IN THE KINGDOM OF GOD

We begin our study with learning. Why, because childhood is the time for learning. As they walk into the classroom for the first time, their only responsibility is to absorb all that the teacher is willing to teach them. They are nothing more than a blank slate waiting to be filled. If the teacher does their job correctly, that child will leave the classroom with his appetite whetted for learning. Fear never enters into the mind of a child who is given answers. With liberty and confidence he asks his questions, knowing that with these answers, he's going to learn something new.

As a child in the Lord, God also encourages us to ask questions. He wants us to be inquisitive about His kingdom and how we can better bring the ways of Heaven here to earth. This was how He approached Jeremiah one day:

> *Call to Me, and I will answer you, and show you great and mighty things, which you do not know.'*
>
> (Jer 33:3)

If there was ever a challenge given by God to us to search out the mysteries of His kingdom, this is it. It is okay not to know some things. It's equally okay to question why. We, as kings and priests (Rev. 1:6), have the legal right to search out the unknown (Prov. 25:2). Equally as important, God would like to give us those answers. There is one prayer that I always pray as I'm entering into a place of worship. I simply ask God to surprise me. Because of my duties as an evangelist, usually I am in service on the average of four to five times a week. This means there are times that God has to do some pretty crazy stuff to get me into the "How did He do that?" stage.

As I was prepared for a three-day revival, I arrived at my hotel and shortly began to pray. Within about 10 minutes, I received a vision from the Lord. To this day, visions are not common in my ministry, and when they happen they are few and far between. From the understanding of the vision, I knew that God was trying to teach me something new. Four different people appeared with various needs. I first saw an Anglo woman with throat and chest problems. I then saw an elderly grandmother, paralyzed in a wheelchair. The third person I saw was a young man having problems with his eyes. Finally, the fourth thing I saw was actually just a red polka dotted dress, and whoever owned this dress suffered with stomach problems. I was so excited that I hurried to the church to see the people I would be ministering to that evening. To my dismay, there was no one in the congregation who looked anywhere near those that I saw in my vision.

I had quickly forgotten about it when, at the first altar call, I was troubled in my spirit. There was an Anglo man (I say Anglo because I usually speak in Hispanic churches) praying who was the cause of my uneasiness. I approached him and asked if there was a woman in his household who suffered with chest and throat problems. With a bewildered look on his face, he responded that I was talking about his wife. Immediately, I felt the Lord tug on my heart, admonishing me to stop the service and begin to minister unto the people. I had never ministered in the altar before I had preached, so I was breaking new ground. I sat everyone down and explained that God wanted to do something special in the house at that moment. With the Pastor's permission, I proceeded and started to ask questions.

I had asked the gentleman to stay at the altar because he was going to stand in for his wife to receive her healing. It was then that I asked if anybody in the congregation knew of an elderly woman, paralyzed in a wheelchair. A young woman who was beginning to cry stood up and proclaimed that I was talking about her grandmother, who had just suffered a stroke and could not walk. She quickly made her way to the altar to stand in line for her. I next asked about the young man with eye problems, and a young man with glasses quickly came to the altar. Finally, with a bit of apprehension, I asked if anybody knew someone with a red polka dotted dress who suffered with stomach problems. Immediately, a young man stood up and blurted that his sister, who was a backslider, had a dress similar to the one that I had described, and that she suffered with those kinds of problems. He gladly made his way up to the altar to stand in for her. We began to pray in the name of Jesus, sending angels of healing to where those people were, and the Lord miraculously healed all of them.

If we could only get out of our ruts and stop limiting God from doing the great and mighty things that He would like to show us, He would. We've just got to be willing to learn new things, and God will take care of the rest.

TRUSTING GOD IN THE KINGDOM

The second characteristic of a child that God uses in His kingdom is trust. Children by far are more trusting than adults. To this day, I am astounded by the love that children have for their parents who have unmercifully abused them. Even as they grow into adults, many of them continue to defend their parents, as if it were a sin to tell it like it really is. Others who have lost that initial trust from abuse also have trust issues when approaching the throne of God.

Our heavenly Father will never abuse us, and we can be confident that as we place ourselves in His hands, everything that is done is in our best interests. That's why He says this in Proverbs:

> *Trust in the LORD with all your heart, and lean not on your own understanding; In all your ways acknowledge Him, and He shall direct your paths.*
>
> (Prov 3:5-6)

He not only wants to be in charge of all the major things in your life, but also the minor things as well. We're so content in handling the minor things, the insignificant things, the things that don't amount to much, that it doesn't even come to mind that if we were to hand it over to Him, He could do a far better job than us. Yet as basic as this concept might be to a child, we as adults fumble and stumble over it as if it were rocket science. Trust Him when you don't know what He is up to. Trust Him when it appears that He has forgotten you. Trust Him when you need strength to make it through the day. Be it big or small, simple or difficult, understandable or not, just trust Him. TRUST HIM! TRUST HIM! TRUST HIM!

When I accepted the challenge to be used by God in a signs and wonders ministry, I was aware that it would be a stretch in many areas, because I was not cut out to be the typical demonstrative, Pentecostal evangelist that folks were accustomed to. From the get go, I could not find anyone within our organization who could mentor me; consequently, I had to find help from the outside. By nature I am not a very trusting person. The hardships in my life did not make it any easier. Trusting God and others has been a painstaking task. I remember a time when I was second-guessing my methods of ministry. The results were similar to others, but how I arrived at them was another thing. Calm, cool, and collected just doesn't cut it in Pentecostal circles. I will never forget the lesson that I learned during this time of indecision.

One year during the Easter season, we had decided to travel several hours to a church that was putting on an Easter extravaganza. This particular church was known for its use of authentic scenery, including animals. The entire production was very professional and Hollywood-like. There came a time in the play when the person playing the role of Jesus went to pray for a blind man. He did it in a way that was not common to us. Without raising his voice, without any fanfare, he quietly prayed for this man in need. I immediately heard the voice of God in my ear, and I will never forget His words. He gently said, "Trust Me, that's really the way I did it." I could not believe what I was hearing. All this time, I was so insecure about how I went about things. Yet God went out of His way to make sure I understood what was most important in His kingdom. Trusting Him was the point that He was trying to make, and how we accomplished our assignments made no difference to Him. I have used that lesson continually to help me in tight spots, especially when my methods have been questioned.

AN ANSWER I DID NOT EXPECT

I was preaching at a junior camp several years ago, and a situation arose when I began to minister unto those on staff. It was late into the night, and I remember being somewhat exhausted. I had approached a woman friend of mine who I knew was in need. I'm always apprehensive to approach someone I know, because it makes it more difficult to discern if what I am hearing is a word of knowledge or something that I was privy to in the past. My friend could not get pregnant for years now into her marriage. Everyone knew that was her petition before God. As I tried to shy away from her, I felt the Lord nudge me and say, TRUST ME! So I took a step of faith and delivered the message that the Lord had impressed upon me. It was somewhat general, so it was not too difficult to interpret. I said, "By the end of this year, you will have the desire of your heart."

When news of the prophecy broke out, the entire camp was ecstatic. The camp ended a few days later and everyone went home happy.

We lived about five or six hours away from each other, which limited fellowshipping maybe to about once or twice a year. I lost track of her, and later found out that she was looking for me. I also found out through the grapevine that she had never given birth, and my assumption was that she was looking for me to give me a piece of her mind. I tried to avoid her as much as possible, but when I caught wind that she was not angry, I began to wonder what she wanted.

We were finally able to meet a couple months later, and what I heard was not what I expected. Although she was never able to physically give birth to a child, she and her husband decided to adopt. The adoption of two children came several years after that time frame that God had promised her blessing. When she hugged me unexpectedly, she was trying to let me know that in fact, my prophecy had come to pass. I was completely flabbergasted by that statement, because I knew that she had not had the children for a very long time. Then she said this: "In the gathering of information at the time of adoption, just about when all was finalized, the authorities allowed us to see the children." They had adopted a brother sister combination. "As I gazed upon my future son coming down the stairwell, the Lord immediately spoke to me and said he is the answer to the prophecy. I really didn't understand where God was coming from until I saw my son's birth certificate. He was born on the last day of the year that the prophecy was to come to pass." God's promise did not come to pass in a way that either of us could anticipate and it caught us completely off guard. I could not believe how God had actually done it, but I sure was glad that he did.

Trusting God at times will mean that we don't understand His ways. Of course, the Lord has given us some insight into that fact through His Word.

> "For My thoughts are not your thoughts, nor are your ways My ways," says the LORD. "For as the heavens are higher than the earth, so are My ways higher than your ways, and My thoughts than your thoughts.
>
> (Isa 55:8-9)

Trusting Him when there is no reason to is a true mark of faith. Taking into account that God has personally spoken to you in one way or another is enough to ride the wave of criticism, ignoring the countless attacks of disapproval.

HUMILITY: A LONG LOST ART

The last characteristic of childhood that we will consider is humility. Children, by nature, are humble. It's amazing how they don't understand rich or poor, smart or not smart, the difference in skin color and the like. It is in these concepts that we as mature adults begin to draw lines and divisions so that we can better complete our agenda. Why is it, on any given day, you can go to any playground in the United States and see children of all races, colors, and creeds playing together? Just one word, it is their humility. You won't find that kind of unity in many of our churches, yet we proclaim to be very, very mature.

When children play on a playground and fight, it's not very long that they will make peace and find themselves out in the yard playing again. There are nations and countries, families and cliques, who have been fighting for so long no one even knows the reason why. Yet it is pride, not humility that will not allow someone to take that first step in making the peace that is needed.

What is even more repulsive is the fact that this spirit has crept into the church. I have been told by many that the reason why folks seeking the Lord do not receive the Holy Ghost is a lack of faith. In all honesty, that has not been my experience. It is really a prideful spirit that does not allow those persons to humble themselves before the presence of God. Sad to say, a proud heart is an abomination unto the Lord. *Everyone proud in heart is an abomination to the LORD;* (Prov 16:5)

That simply means that he hates pride and will not endure it. *The one who has a haughty look and a proud heart, him I will not endure.* (Ps 101:5)

The greatest lesson that I learned about humility came by way of a four-year-old little girl. A few years back, my son and I made a trip out of state during the Easter holidays. For several months before the revival, the Pastor went out of his way to prepare the people for a great outpouring of God's Spirit through signs and wonders.

Upon our arrival the first day, you could sense the congregation's anticipation of great things to come. Included in the number of those waiting for their miracle was a six year old blind girl.

That night during the altar call, something happened that angered the Lord. Through a word of knowledge, the Lord informed me that the woman I was ministering to had lied. It wasn't until after the service that we found out that this woman was in actuality a Pastor's wife, from one of the neighboring churches. Her lies incensed the Lord so much that for the next two days, He refused to heal anyone. I had never encountered a situation like this, but neither was I going to go against God's wishes. It was on the final day of the revival that I was released to pray for the sick. Unfortunately, the little blind girl was not in attendance. It was a sunrise service on Easter morning, with only the local congregation attending. I don't know if the young lady was just asleep or if in fact was not there, but she missed out because the Lord unleashed His glory in that service and healed many. At the outset of the final service, the Lord had impressed me to reserve all ministering to those who were visiting. That would mean that the little girl who missed out in the morning would not have a similar opportunity for healing, because her parents were part of that local congregation.

A line of sick people made their way up to the altar, and one by one I began to pray for their needs. At the end of the line, out of the corner of my eye, I saw a woman in a wheelchair. She had a tank of oxygen hanging from the back of the chair, with plastic tubes running up her nose. Little by little, as I made my way closer to her, I could sense that the faith of the entire congregation was growing because everybody in line received their healing. When I finally got to her, I inquired why she needed the oxygen. She responded to me that because of a tumor in her chest that was pressing against her lung, she could not breathe without the use of the oxygen. I wanted to know where her faith was at the moment, so I asked her if she believed God could heal her at that moment. She replied with a resounding, "You better believe it."

That genuinely excited me, because that type of response is not very common in the church. It is that type of response that an evangelist must take advantage of, because it is that kind of faith that will produce miracles. Her response was so childlike that I began to feed off of her faith. I then asked her if, after the prayer when God healed her, as a sign of her healing, she would be willing to stand up. I asked her this not only to confirm her healing, but that it would also be a sign to the rest of the congregation that God had completed this miracle. I finally told her this: "I'm not even going to lay my hands on you, I'm just going to point my finger and declare your healing in the name of Jesus." It didn't make a difference to her, because as far as she was concerned, once I was done praying, she was going to have her answer.

I prayed a short prayer, and once I finished, immediately she stood up. The tumor had disappeared instantaneously and she kept on tapping her chest to see if she could find it. When I asked her if the tubes up her nose were still necessary, she said no, and gleefully removed them. I then took her by the hand and we began to take a victory march around the church. The power of God fell in such a glorious way that the entire congregation was rejoicing in the Spirit. When we got back to the front, I had decided that it was a good time to leave the remainder of the service in the hands of the Pastor. Any evangelist worth his weight in salt knows that his job is done when the glory of God has filled the house, and that day the mission was accomplished.

I went back up to the platform to pray, but in reality I wasn't really praying. I began to hear the shouts and cries of the people and I just wanted to soak up the moment. It was at this time that pride began to creep into my heart. I also was listening to what the people were saying about me and how they had never seen God use a man quite so powerfully as they had that weekend. My head continued to grow with one of the characteristics that God hates most: pride. Unfortunately for me, I was about to be humbled by God. In His distaste for what I had allowed in my heart, he was going to make sure that it wasn't going to stay there.

When I got up from prayer, waiting for me at the foot of the platform was the little blind girl, motioning to me to come to her. I tried to convince her that my time of ministry had been completed, but she wouldn't take no for an answer. I really didn't want to minister to her because I knew that she was blind, and in that point in time of my ministry, the gift of healing the eyes, for whatever reason, had not been perfected. For those of you who don't know, there is not only one gift of healing, there are many. And as a servant of God continues to use what God has given to him, it has the opportunity to continue to grow into perfection. Until that point comes, there is a lot of hit and miss. I really didn't want to put a damper on what God had already done, so I was trying to convince her that praying for her condition was out of the question. She still would not take no for an answer. I eventually succumbed to her will and began to pray with not much hope for success.

However, when I turned around I saw something that I did not expect. Her lazy eye that was causing the blindness all of a sudden stopped moving. The pride in me actually incensed me. I knew that there was a healing going on, but because I could not take credit for it, it only made me more angry. We had done some testing to confirm the miracle, and when the dust settled, I had to admit that she could see. I almost lost out on experiencing the greatest miracle that God had done in my ministry, because of my pride.

A FOUR YEAR OLD'S FAITH

Do you want to know why this blind girl got healed? It was her faith, of course, that opened the windows of Heaven for this miracle. Did you ever wonder where her faith came from? Her faith came from the heart of her younger sister, who was only four years old. I was told after the fact that the younger sister would come knocking on her sister's door, repeating this phrase about every 10 minutes. "When the man of God comes to our church, God is going to heal you." Every 10 minutes, every day, for three months, she would not stop.

I can just about discern the thoughts of many readers right now. Many of you are thinking, of course a little girl at that age makes unbelievable statements like that. She doesn't know any better. She doesn't understand that there are times when God just doesn't heal, and for her everything is possible. That's exactly my point. Unless we become as little children who can believe God for the impossible, we are never going to see the glory of God fill our congregations. It is a childlike faith that believes everything that will allow God be God.

If an altar call was to be made at this moment, would you humble yourself to the point where you would be willing to allow God to teach you things in His Spirit that you know nothing of? Would you be willing to trust Him with all of your life, even if He doesn't explain what He is doing? Only a childlike faith would allow God that kind of control. Are you willing?

Chapter 4
WHERE IS YOUR FAITH?

*Now faith is the substance of things hoped for,
the evidence of things not seen.*

(Heb 11:1)

But He said to them, "Where is your faith?"

(Luke 8:25)

One of the most controversial, if not misunderstood, concepts of the Bible is faith. Because of its misuse and abuse in the past, people are not so willing to step out on a limb and risk their reputations by declaring outrageous statements that are not going to come to pass. To add insult to injury, those who work in the realm of faith have tried to keep it so mysterious, spooky, and only understandable to a select few, that the rest of us simply raise our hands in futility and give up. But the biggest error that I have heard many a preacher make in explaining faith is the inability to distinguish it from hope. Because the two are similar in many ways, it is assumed that they are one and the same, and yet their differences are like night and day.

HOPE: LOOKING TO THE FUTURE

On the surface, faith and hope appear the same because they both put trust in things that cannot be seen. Whether you are waiting for a physical healing, whether God has promised a financial blessing, or even as a parent you are waiting on God for the salvation of one of your children, these things are not readily visible by the naked eye. Now let's discuss where the two begin to separate.

Hope always looks to the future and must be patient. *But if we hope for what we do not see, we eagerly wait for it with perseverance.* (Rom 8:25) Persevering in times of waiting is easier said than done. The longer our answer is prolonged, the easier it is for us to give up hope. Time and time again, many have said in despair that after receiving a promise from God, they truly believed He could make it come to pass, but it was just that they did not think it would take so long. Their perseverance and patience had not only begun to wane, they were consequently making them sick. How true the words of Solomon when he said: *Hope deferred makes the heart sick....* (Prov 13:12). By this time you're probably wondering, "What's the use of hoping in the first place if it's not going to bring the solution to my problem?" I will answer that question after I explain what faith really is and how the two work together.

FAITH: IT'S ALL ABOUT RIGHT NOW

The glaring difference about faith compared to hope is that faith doesn't have the time to wait. Neither can it be patient. Faith is all about "right now." It will take the hope of the future, convert it into the daily steps needed to get an answer, and put it into action. Faith doesn't just sit there, it moves. At this point, let me put a handle on the two concepts, bring them together and show you how God uses both to help us receive from Him.

This is the process that God uses to provide for His children. When the Lord has chosen to use time in order for His promise to come to pass, we will use hope in our waiting to sustain us. But at the time that the Lord is ready to open His hands of provision, we must convert our hope into faith. This is where most of us fail the test. Too many in the kingdom say that they are waiting on God in faith. That's impossible, because faith doesn't wait. In actuality, they are waiting in hope. Until they are able to convert their hope into faith, they will wait until the end of time, because God always responds to faith.

How then do we make this conversion? In an earlier chapter, I explained how faith comes by hearing (Rom.10: 17). When God is ready to move, He will specifically instruct us as to what must be done in order to receive. That rhema (i.e., a specific word, for a specific person, for a specific time) put into action will always bring the desired results. Faith is not some cloudy, mysterious, abstract concept that cannot be understood or found. Faith is simply listening to the word of God, written or spoken, obeying it and putting it into action. It is nothing more and nothing less. It is so easy that even a child can put this into practice (see Chapter 3).

When I come to this part of explaining the difference between faith and hope, there is always one question that people are dying to ask. They inquisitively inquire, "How can you be sure that what you are hearing or feeling impressed of God is really God?" The answer that I continue to give is this.

I AM NEVER SURE. If there were a 100% surety that what I am hearing from God is truly Him, then my responding to Him would not need faith. Let me calm your nerves a bit and share a couple of factors involved that happen every time God wants me to move in faith.

1. He will ask of me something that I have never done, or have rarely done.

2. Upon receiving my instructions from God, the enemy immediately comes to intimidate me with fear.

The knowledge of these things does not remove the fear; neither does it make my assignments any easier. Consequently, I make a decision to move by faith, and God always comes to the rescue.

I learned a great lesson from CSI (crime scene investigators). When arriving at a crime scene, although there are various people who have witnessed the crime, the main focus of the CSI is on the evidence. Why, because the evidence, unlike people, never lies. It is reliable, dependable, and consistent. The evidence never wavers or succumbs to pressure. It is always the same. I used this line of thinking in applying it to the word of God. After a period of time waiting in hope, God then begins to speak our blessing into existence through His rhema. At that time when we receive His word, it becomes the substance, the matter, the material tangible enough that we can latch onto it, putting it into action to unleash His glory. Those circumstances or situations may tempt us to stray away from what we have heard from God, yet His word is always reliable, dependable, and consistent. It never wavers or succumbs to pressure of people. Our faith truly is the evidence of things not seen.

THE MIRACLE AT THE POOL

One day as Jesus walked by the pool of Bethesda, He encountered a paralytic man waiting for his healing. He sat there in hope because he believed that the tradition of the Jews regarding healing was true. It said that anyone who jumped into the pool first after an angel from Heaven descended to trouble the water would receive their healing. Jesus, I'm sure knowing the tradition, approached him with this question. *Do you want to be made well?* (John 5: 6) I will get to his response in just a minute, but I would like to speculate a moment on perhaps what he (the paralytic) was thinking. You know as well as I do that in responding to questions, we don't always say what we think. By the way he responded to the Lord, somewhat politically correct, I wonder what he was really thinking. "What kind of question was that? This guy must be from out of town; doesn't he know that all the sick folk gather around this pool, waiting to be healed? I'm not here to get a tan, you know." But look at the words that actually come out of his mouth.

The sick man answered Him, "Sir, I have no man to put me into the pool when the water is stirred up; but while I am coming, another steps down before me."

(John 5:7)

His hope was in getting into the pool first; because that's the only way he knew that he could be healed. The problem with this was that that was not the question Jesus asked. The Lord's question could have been answered with a simple "yes" or "no." Jesus was not interested as to why he had not been healed; He was only interested in knowing if he still wanted it. In these times, as the Lord ventures out to ask us the same question, our response to Him is much the same. Instead of answering "yes" or "no," we ramble on and on with our reasons and our excuses why we are not healed. There are moments we will go back in time to the aches and pains that our parents, grandparents, and even great-grandparents suffered to justify that what we are feeling today just runs in the family. Yet again, that's neither here nor there to Him. He just wants to know if we would like to receive our healing today.

This is where our experience in God, or lack thereof, plays a big part. So many times we limit God in performing miracles by what we know or have experienced. We are so traditional in so many ways that when God will begin to speak to us in a way in which we are not accustomed, we discount it as not being the voice of God. When I go out to minister at a church, I will purposely not use anointing oil to pray for the sick. I don't do this because I do not believe in this practice, however, my goal in that service is to show the people of God that there is more than one way that the Lord can heal. I will go as far as not even praying for them, to help them understand that this method is biblical as well. Every time I ask someone if they believe God could heal them if I do not pray for them, you should see the cockeyed looks I get. They think it's a trick question.

Let's go back to this paralytic man and how Jesus ministered to him, to help you see that my methods aren't as a wacky as you think.

> *"Jesus said to him, "Rise, take up your bed and walk."*
>
> (John 5:8)

Where is the prayer in that statement? It appears to me that Jesus just looked him straight in the eye and declared his healing. For years, I had been doing this, not even realizing that what I was doing was biblical, yet I was highly criticized for it. The fact that people were getting healed left and right did not matter, because I wasn't doing it like everybody else.

Again, let us go back to the paralytic's dilemma to consider the same questions that he had on that day. Remember, Jesus had just commanded him to get up. What would he do with that order? What kind of decisions did he have to make?

1. Who was this man making these crazy orders?

2. Why was He changing the way people got healed?

3. Was this lawful to be done on the Sabbath?

First of all, he had probably never seen Jesus before in his life, nor heard of Him. What gave Him the authority to make these kinds of requests? The Lord then was asking him to completely change the way they had been taught to receive a blessing that he so desperately needed. Finally, the paralytic man knew that no work should be done on the Sabbath. It was designed by God as a day of rest. Would he be breaking a law that would ultimately condemn him to hell? What would be the virtue of being physically healed if, when in eternity, it meant spending that time without God? Only a rhema from God would allow a person to take that kind of risk. What he had heard that day and how Jesus, in His authority, had said it was enough for him to take that risk. He then took that word, put it into action, and ran with it. What a magnificent show of faith from a man who we least expected it from.

GROWING IN FAITH: A CONTINUAL LEARNING

The understanding of faith and its use in everyday life has been a continual learning process for me. I had to undo the rigid checks and balances philosophies that I was taught in the business world. Faith in that arena was so nonexistent; it was all about the bottom line. Logic was religiously pursued, and anything less than that was discarded.

One such lesson of faith comes to mind when the Lord began to deal with me when my right leg began to lose muscle mass. While it wasn't at all painful, there was a great weakening in the leg. To this day, the doctors have not been able to figure out what is going on. Some say it's due to complications of diabetes; others have gone to the other extreme, believing that the polio that had been dormant in my body for over 40 years has slowly returned. The Lord has been somewhat mute in responding to the whys of my condition as well.

I have already written that every need God would like to solve that will be answered over a period of time always begins with hope. To satisfy that requirement, the Lord gave me a word. If I were to begin a walking program, He would heal me while I was walking. It seemed like a doable request, so I began to walk. Of course, because there was no specific time frame included in that word, I was deeply disappointed when the answer did not come quickly. The days turned to weeks, the weeks to months, and still no healing.

One day while I was walking, I received new instructions. "It's time to run," said the Lord. Run? I was still having difficulty walking, much less running.

As I scoffed at His demand, he said it again. "Run."

"Come on, God," I responded, "you've got to be kidding, you know I can't run."

"Come on, run."

I was somewhat miffed at His persistence, so I decided to get spiritual. "Didn't you tell me in your word that you were going to heal me while I was WALKING?" There was no response, yet I knew I wasn't going to win this argument, so I humbled myself and attempted to run. Only after about 10 seconds, my right leg gave in and I almost fell down. I gazed up into the sky, pointing my finger, and blurted out, YOU SEE!

The Lord did not respond to my challenge, calmly waiting until I cooled down. He then asked me to try it again. Although I was not in agreement to give it another try, there was something in my spirit that said *there is a lesson for you in this, give it your best shot.* I marked my watch, began to jog again, and this time to my surprise I was able to go for 30 seconds without my leg collapsing.

I continued walking for several minutes when the Lord came one last time and said, "Do it again."

This time, without hesitation I began to jog, and lo and behold, when I looked at my watch again, I had been running for a minute and 20 seconds. I understand that that is not a very long period of time; even so, I could build upon that act of faith so that my leg could be completely healed. Subsequent to that time, I have continued to increase my running time to over an hour, something that had never been accomplished before. (Note to reader: the leg is still not healed, I will explain in a later chapter.)

WHAT DOES THE EVIDENCE SAY?

The lies from the enemy we have accepted that hinder us from taking such steps of faith are two-pronged. The first lie comes from the accusation that we have no faith at all. It is so readily accepted because many times, we don't even know what faith is to begin with. But in times of indecision, we can always go to His word, because it is our evidence, and the evidence never lies.

> *...think soberly, as God has dealt to each one a measure of faith.*
>
> (Rom 12:3)

The apostle tells us that God has given each and every one of us a measure of faith so that we might be able to think in our right mind. No one in His kingdom has been excluded, because the evidence tells us so. The second lie from our adversary is somewhat more cunning in that although he admits that the Scripture in Romans is true, the faith that we do have is not enough to produce the answer that we need. Again, when these false accusations are being made, all we need to do is go back to the evidence. What kind of faith is needed to move the mountains in our life?

> *So Jesus said to them, "... if you have faith as a mustard seed, you will say to this mountain, 'Move from here to there,' and it will move; and nothing will be impossible for you.*
>
> (Matt 17:20)

If we are not receiving answers from God, it's not His fault. If moving the mountains of our lives only requires

64

faith the size of a mustard seed, and we are still not receiving, that must mean that we are not putting our faith into action. The evidence in this case is quite clear that the windows of Heaven will open to those who will extend their hands to Him in faith.

Over the years, I have exhausted myself trying to understand why we, as the children of God, are not putting our faith into action. Understanding that for generations there had been confusion between hope and faith had somewhat calmed my nerves. Needless to say, faith is not what the church of today lives by. Truth be told, the blessings of God have been ever so abundant that in many cases, it's not needful to move in the realm of faith. Our homes and families, our finances, even our health, are secured by elements other than God. Perceiving that the condition of the church will only deteriorate, it's not shocking to believe the words of Jesus when He said: *Nevertheless, when the Son of Man comes, will He really find faith on the earth?"* (Luke 18:8).

PUTTING FAITH IN THE WRONG PERSON

Listen to what happened to a woman and her daughter during a mission's trip that I took to Mexico. The Lord had sent me to the same place twice in one year, Tecoman, Mexico. On the last day of my first visit, I encountered a young lady wearing braces on both legs. I found out that her right leg was shorter than the left. The bone of her hip was out of position, moving towards her back. Because of the unevenness of the legs, she was forced to wear braces on both legs, being separated by a rod. Due to the restriction of the braces, she could not put one foot in front of the other as she walked.

She struggled a great deal to get around. When I felt

impressed to pray for her healing, I knew it was God because immediately the enemy began to terrorize me with fear. He knew that I knew I had never prayed for somebody in that condition.

What made matters worse was that on the previous night, I chickened out and did not pray for this little girl. Knowing that I had been given a second chance, I stepped out by faith, leaving the fear behind me. I sat the young lady down and took off the braces. I instructed her to extend out both legs and to leave them like that while we prayed. After a brief prayer, I stood her up. It did not appear as if anything had miraculously happened during the prayer. But as I stood her up again, this time she wasn't bent over to one side, she stood straight up. The bone that was out of place also moved so that her body was in complete alignment. I asked her if she could walk, but because she was so used to using the braces, her initial attempts were feeble at most. She walked ever so gently. Remember that she was not used to putting one foot in front of the other. I let her sit down because she looked somewhat exhausted. The service was now starting to wind down, and the Pastor picked up a final love offering. As her mama gave her something to place in the offering basket, something incredible happened.

The young lady was still walking as she had when she first received her healing. But as the money that she deposited in the basket left her hand, she began to convert her hope into faith. She began to dash through the congregation as an Olympic sprinter would for his country. Round and round and round she went as the glory of God entered into the sanctuary. I was greatly amused by the conga line that she had formed with the other children. She put the braces on her head as if it were a headdress that a dancer would wear, and the children behind her danced the night away. She composed a little tune that was repeated over and over. "I don't have to go Guadalajara." Guadalajara was the city that she visited when she went to the doctor. I asked her mom to go back to the doctor so that they could confirm what God had done, so that He might receive all of the glory. She agreed that she would.

When I returned to Tecoman eight months later, I gazed out into the crowd, looking for the little girl, but she was nowhere to be found. I inquired of the Pastor for her, but he was embarrassed to say that she and her mama no longer attended. When I continued to ask him why, he told me, "Do you remember how you asked the mother to go back and see the doctor, so that they could confirm this healing that God had performed?" "Of course," I said.

He continued by saying, "That's exactly what she did. When they arrived in Guadalajara and entered into the doctor's office, the young lady was still playing with the apparatus on top of her head. When the doctors came out to greet them and saw her playing, in horror and disbelief they began to scold the mother. They said, 'What in the world is wrong with you? Don't you know the harm that you have done by taking off those braces? Put them back on immediately or we will not only take away your child, we will put you in jail so that you will never ever see her again.' Startled by their reaction, she did what she was told and walked out. In two months time, everything that the Lord had performed that day was undone. The young lady was then forced to wear the braces that she hated so much. Realizing that she had made a mistake, the mother's pride would not allow her to return to the church."

WHY GOD CHOOSES TO USE DOCTORS

I have written this testimony, not with the intention of degrading anything that those in medicine have accomplished. There have been great discoveries in medicine that I believe have been God inspired. How so? God in His wisdom understood that in this time and place, living by faith would be a stretch even for those in the church (See Luke 18:8). So He has opened up the minds of doctors and researchers alike to discover treatments and medicine that will bring healing to our bodies.

He fully understood that many would not accept His provision that could only be provided through faith, so He engineered another way. There would, of course, be conditions that we would not have to deal with when being healed by God. Because the medical profession is a practice, meaning that at times they don't know what they are doing, consequently we have to deal with side effects. On the other hand the healing that is received from Heaven is genuine, pure, and indisputable, with no side effects whatsoever. It's incredible to believe that most people today choose the lesser provision when God's provision is not only superior, it's also free.

Moving people out of their comfort zones into the realm of faith, in their eyes, is not worth it. It's just too hard. No one really ever likes change, especially one that will include losing control of their lives. Nonetheless, it's never too hard; it's just God's way. That's what we'll focus on in the next chapter.

Chapter 5
IT'S JUST TOO HARD

Thou therefore endure hardness, as a good soldier of Jesus Christ.

(2 Tim 2:3)

As the foundation of this chapter, I would like to take some time defining the word *hardness*. As **Webster's Dictionary** says, hardness is something that is high in content, in degree, or amount. Most hard liquor we find today is high in alcohol. If water is high in chemicals, it will not allow cleansing so easily, thus it is considered hard water. When we contemplate hard problems, they are regarded as ones that will demand more of our effort to reach solutions that are not easily found. At times, the problems before us have the appearance of being insurmountable. The harshness, severity and discomfort brought about by these problems will be difficult to understand or explain. In my first book, **An Evil Day** (chapter 9), I related a story about the untimely death of a five-year-old friend of my daughter, Stephanie.

To this day, it is still hard to fathom how God would permit such a tragedy to occur. I'm sure that the parents of Stephen, the little boy who died, would agree as well. These kinds of uncertainties will weigh heavily on our mind. They are the fiery darts that will be dodged if at all possible.

Suffice it to say, although these examples make it a bit more unbelievable, there are benefits in hardness. Any artist will agree that the various degrees of hardness in their pencils are what bring out the detail and beauty in their sketches. We find that when the lead is soft, it will produce a darker shade.

In contrast, when the lead is harder it will produce a lighter shade. If we put this into the terms of living for Christ, we will find that living a soft life will not produce much blessing. If our serving God is soft, being lazy, immature, and carnal, we will always be in the dark. The secrets and the mysteries of the Gospel will stay hidden, and our growth in Him will be minimal. On the other hand, if our serving of God is hard with a concerted, focused, and driven effort, embracing it as a fine treasure, the light shone on us will illuminate our pathway to greater wisdom and understanding in the kingdom.

> *Wisdom is the principal thing; therefore get wisdom. And in all your getting, get understanding. Exalt her, and she will promote you; She will bring you honor, when you embrace her. She will place on your head an ornament of grace; a crown of glory she will deliver to you. "*
>
> (Prov 4:7-9)

OUR INDENITY

When we endure the hardness of Satan's attacks, we in turn will be hardened in Christ. The armor of our protection will not only become invincible, but we will shine with a brightness that identifies us with the Army of the Lord. We will be brought into the light of life if we will follow his lead.

> *Then Jesus spoke to them again, saying, "I am the light of the world. He who follows Me shall not walk in darkness, but have the light of life."*
> (John 8:12)

If there's one thing that Satan cannot stand, it is the light. The Prince of Darkness is exposed in the light. It is the light that uncovers his diabolical plans. Much like rodents and cockroaches that take advantage of the darkness to run wild, creating havoc, Satan, too, runs when the light is turned on.

> *For everyone practicing evil hates the light and does not come to the light, lest his deeds should be exposed But he who does the truth comes to the light, that his deeds may be clearly seen, that they have been done in God."*
> (John 3:20-21)

AN EYE OPENING EXPERIENCE

When I went to Las Vegas for the first time, I was sent there by my employer for a computer convention. I was so apprehensive upon my arrival because of all of the stories that I had heard of "Sin City." During the day, there were periods of time where we were allowed to go outside the convention center for a break. As I gazed out onto Las Vegas Blvd., admiring the beautiful hotels and casinos, I could not figure out what the big deal was about Las Vegas. It appeared like any other normal metropolis with people walking the streets, carrying on their business, and the debauchery that was supposedly running rampant day and night was nowhere to be found. I began to think that what I had heard was completely overblown.

I saw casinos like "Circus Circus" that were dedicated to the enjoyment of all the family. I was told that Las Vegas was continuing to change to attract more families, and that to a greater extent, casinos for the most part were becoming more family-friendly. I was beginning to soften my stance on "the city that never sleeps" when slowly the sun began to set. When the seminars were over, we were given the nights off, so we hit the strip to see what was going on. It was then that I understood why this city had the reputation that it had. Immediately I felt evilness come over me.

As I glanced around me, I noticed that the people were dressed differently, especially the ladies, much more provocative. The carefree spirit led to unbridled kissing, hugging, and touching.

There were men on street corners handing out flyers to the local whorehouses, with no one seeming to care. The children I saw throughout the day were replaced by underage drunken teenagers who were looking for a good time. It was the night that drew out all of this craziness. It was the night that was able to hide what was not lawful, and it was the night that helped coin the phrase "whatever happens in Vegas stays in Vegas."

It is not surprising then that Satan uses the night to do his best work. Nevertheless, where darkness reigns, light shines brighter. We are encouraged to cast off the works of the darkness by enduring, and only by enduring will our armor shine brightly.

> *The night is far spent, the day is at hand. Therefore let us cast off the works of darkness, and let us put on the armor of light.*
>
> (Rom 13:12)

If we are to endure hardness as the Scripture says, so that our armor of light will be able to protect us, we must come to realize that the fight that we are engaged in is a spiritual one.

> *For we do not wrestle against flesh and blood, but against principalities, against powers, against the rulers of the darkness of this age, against spiritual hosts of wickedness in the heavenly places.*
>
> (Eph 6:12)

SATAN'S HIGHLY ORGANIZED ARMY

This Scripture helps us to understand that the onslaught of the devil is highly organized. He is a master strategist with a master plan. His schemes are well thought out and have been used for thousands of years to perfect them. His rank and file are devoted to one single purpose, and that is to utterly destroy those who have been assigned to them. I can even go one step further to believe that he will do everything in his power to devastate you, with no chance of you getting back up. For this reason he fights dirty, knowing that all is fair in love and war, and this truly is war.

Why is he so extremely motivated, you might say? That's an easy question to answer, because there is an ... *everlasting fire prepared for the devil and his angels:* (Matt 25:41). Hell was not originally prepared for you and me; it was prepared as the final judgment place in eternity both for Satan and his demons. Because misery loves company, Satan has decided to take as many with him as possible. It stands to reason that he would try to flood your mind with the hardest water imaginable. The water that he produces is filled with all kinds of grief including lies, deceit, sorrow, sickness, and loss. This water is so hard that once it has fully penetrated people's resolve, they can be thoroughly overwhelmed by its impact.

By the sound of it, it would appear that we stand no chance against this high octane fighting machine. Bear in mind this little statistic. For every demon assigned to you to make your life miserable, there are two angels. To make matters more stressful for these demons, they are being asked to cover more territory without being given any more help. The birthrate continues to grow so rapidly each day that they (the demons) are working overtime just to keep up. On top of that, the word of God encourages us by jogging our memory to this awesome fact,

> *So shall they fear the name of the LORD from the west, and His glory from the rising of the sun; When the enemy comes in like a flood, the Spirit of the LORD will lift up a standard against him.*
>
> (Isa 59:19)

It needn't matter if you live on the sunny beaches of California in the West or you make your abode in the overcrowded cities of China in the East, God's got your back. The Scriptures literally say that once the enemy comes at us like a flood and or river **(Strong's Dictionary)** the Spirit of the Lord comes in like a whirlwind, scaring him away as he runs and hides.

What force or power could have that kind of an affect upon the most evil mastermind ever created when he imposes himself upon us with guns blazing?

It could only be the rivers of God.

"He who believes in Me, as the Scripture has said, out of his heart will flow rivers of living water."

(John 7:38)

THE RIVERS OF GOD

When a Spirit-filled believer calls on the name of Jesus, it creates a clash of the titans, the rivers of living water versus the rivers of Satan. This is really not a fair fight, because God's water is harder than Satan's. The chemical makeup of Satan's water is no match for God's love, mercy, grace, and forgiveness. Therefore,...

No weapon formed against you shall prosper
(Isa 54:17).

In actuality, there is a much greater spiritual significance that is brought to Satan's attention when the rivers of life are released. Water will forever always remind him of Calvary. *But one of the soldiers pierced His side with a spear, and immediately blood and water came out.* (John 19:34) The focus of this Scripture is usually on the blood, and rightfully so. We must never forget the precious blood that bought our redemption and salvation through the forgiveness of our sins. But in the redemption plan, God also left us a footnote that through His Spirit, that water of regeneration would also help us to overpower our enemy. The rivers of living water that flow through us out of our heart connect us to Jesus at Calvary. You see, when His heart burst from being broken, that was in effect what allowed the blood and water to flow out of His side. Because of Calvary, we too can lift up a standard against Satan, and there's nothing he can do about it.

WE ARE HAND PICKED BY GOD

We now move on to the rest of the Scriptures that talk about being a good soldier. A good soldier, to begin with, is servant-minded. All of his thoughts, ideas, opinions, desires, and dreams, are put on hold. In his mind, he has been commissioned to serve unreservedly, even unto death.

As a soldier in Christ's army, he understands that he has been hand-picked by God, which in turn brings excitement and emotion which, in remembrance of such, will benefit him in times of war.

You did not choose Me, but I chose you and appointed you that you should go and bear fruit, and that your fruit should remain, that whatever you ask the Father in My name He may give you.

(John 15:16)

There have been various times in my life when being hand-picked had a great influence. As a sixth-grader in elementary school, I was the only one in the district allowed to play in the junior high band, first chair at that. Then as a ninth-grader in junior high, I was allowed to practice with the varsity football team at our local high school. While in high school, I was the only junior to be selected on the all Southern California football team. Each time I heard my name selected, I felt very special. To know that I was the only one to be chosen was not only humbling, but I considered each one a great honor. The impact was such that it became the ultimate motivator to give it my best shot. I was going to do everything in my power to make the people who had chosen me believe that they had made the right choice.

That is how we must view our being chosen by God. The Master of the universe never makes mistakes; neither does He make decisions by being coerced. He knows what He wants, knows where to find it, and how to get it. Being chosen by Him was not an afterthought; He knew exactly what He was doing.

Taking that into consideration, don't you believe that we owe it to ourselves to give Him our best? If enduring hardships is what it takes, then so be it.

For this reason, a good soldier will not entangle himself with the cares of this life, meaning he will not entwine himself, get tied up, or get off-track. He wants to be pleasing to the one who chose him in the first place (2 Tim. 2:4). He understands at the get-go that he will be placed in precarious situations, ones that will stretch his faith to the max. Such situations won't matter to him because he knows that by extending his faith in these matters, he will be found pleasing in the sight of God.

But without faith it is impossible to please Him, for he who comes to God must believe that He is, and that He is a rewarder of those who diligently seek Him.

(Heb 11:6)

That's right! God is looking for soldiers who will serve Him HARD, or as the Scripture above would put it, *diligently.* God's hand of provision is always open to those who make the extra effort to keep Him Lord in their lives.

That in turn brings God to a place of bragging on us. These so-called "endurers" in the faith are so few that when the Lord finds ones sprinkled amongst the rest of His children, He takes the opportunity to boast. That's exactly what happened when the Lord and Satan had a conversation one day.

Then the LORD said to Satan, "Have you considered My servant Job, that there is none like him on the earth, a blameless and upright man, one who fears God and shuns evil?"

(Job 1:8)

JOB ENDURES HARDNESS

Even before Job had an opportunity to endure hardness, God begins to lay claims to this man's integrity. While in the middle of Job's suffering, after the loss of his family, the Lord persists in bragging on. The Lord is pretty calm in His assessment of the situation because He already knows the outcome. Job didn't know it yet, but his enduring hardness would eventually bring him to victory. That's the kind of confidence the Lord has in us. It may appear that we are going down for the count, nevertheless

He prides Himself in the fact that He... *calls those things which do not exist as though they did;* (Rom 4:17).

He can lay the wood on the accuser of the saints before the fact because He knows... *he who endures to the end shall be saved.* (Matt 24:13)

The decision then to endure is ultimately ours. The Lord will only recruit those with the willingness to fight. If the cost is not counted before the fight begins, then when hardness and/or hard times come, the battle will be lost. When a soldier of Christ cannot endure hardness and decides to quit, it's usually because he hasn't taken the time to consider the consequences of his decision. Because suffering has the tendency to dull our discerning capabilities, rash decisions are made in the heat of the battle. It is when all is said and done, and we have the opportunity to survey the situation more discreetly that we come to the conclusion that we should have kept on going.

I found out that people who cannot endure hardness are those that not only lose out on God, but lose out on their destiny as well. Although the Spirit in them begins to dry and eventually die, there are also physical repercussions to consider. Physically, the heart in many cases begins to shrivel from overwork and eventually ceases to function. What is an even greater tragedy is the fact that that person could not endure, and as a result never became the man or woman of God that the Lord initially had planned for them to be.

LOSING OUT ON HIS DESTINY

My dad was a vivacious kind of guy. He lived life to the fullest and did everything with pizzazz. His life was one exclamation point after another. If you were to look in the dictionary under the word flashy, you would find a picture of him plastered in the middle. His charismatic personality had a tendency to draw people to him constantly. He used his God-given gifts to the fullest by becoming one of the greatest salesmen that I have ever known. He was so good that he could sell an air conditioner to an Eskimo in the deepest of winter. My admiration for him and his skills grew when I had the opportunity to work for him in the furniture store that he owned. Every day for four years, I watched closely as he managed, maneuvered, and manipulated his way to a sale. No one and nothing ever got by him. Whatever language was more comfortable for those he was dealing with, that was what he would speak. I was utterly fascinated when, in dealing with Latino people from various countries, his accent in Spanish would also change to the accent that they spoke with. He was hilarious.

I never knew that he had a call of God on his life, one that included a preaching ministry. In the back of my mind, I always felt that because of his flair for the dramatic, he would make a great preacher in our church, especially because we were Pentecostal. It wasn't until we had a heart to heart talk that I had found out. We sat down one day so that I could inform him that I was no longer interested in taking over the business once he retired. I had received a call to preach and I wanted to dedicate the rest of my life to this endeavor. I thought he was going to be greatly disappointed at the hearing of the bad news, but instead his eyes welled up with tears and he got very emotional. He said, "Son, as disappointed as I am knowing that I will not be able to turn over my business to you, I could not be any prouder." It was then that he admitted there was a time that he, too, had a call of God upon his life. His call never came to fulfillment.

When I was five years old, my dad left the home and my parents divorced. He had entangled himself in the cares of life and a great career that provided well for him. With so much residual income at his disposal, material things became more important than God. He was talented enough to get by, so much so that he was initiated to the ministry without setting much time aside for God. His downfall came when he continued to try to fight a spiritual fight in the flesh. Little by little, his resistance was being broken down by the hardness of life.

When push came to shove, he couldn't handle the pressure. He committed adultery and left God and his family, but also his destiny.

His death was both sudden and tragic in that a heart attack killed him. It was tragic in the sense that the heart attack was not severe enough to cause death. But the autopsy showed something that was entirely unexpected. His heart had shriveled and was completely dry. This 51-year-old man who was so full of life had the heart of a 70-year-old. When God's Spirit began to dry up in him, so did his heart. Never did he consider that turning away from God would have physical repercussions. If only he could have endured.

Let's take one last look at enduring hardness. Its literal translation is to suffer afflictions together with God. It may appear that you're alone in all of this, but in reality when we suffer, He suffers right along with us. The hurt, the disappointment, the pain, are just as real to Him as they are to us. He makes time to be sure that every little bit of discomfort on our part is documented so that we cannot accuse Him of neglect. Therefore, if He can endure, so can we. Our reward will far outweigh our decision not

81

to endure.

> *Blessed is the man who endures temptation; for when he has been approved, he will receive the crown of life which the Lord has promised to those who love Him.*

(James 1:12)

Chapter 6
WANTED: DEAD, NOT ALIVE

For to me, to live is Christ, and to die is gain.
(Phil 1:21)

Most assuredly, I say to you, unless a grain of wheat falls into the ground and dies, it remains alone; but if it dies, it produces much grain.
(John 12:24)

We have a fascination with life that goes without saying. We will avoid it and anything that has to do with it like the plague. For many, the mysteriousness and uncertainty of death is better left alone, and although they see death all around them, they would rather believe that death's call will not come knocking on their door.

I recall a friend recounting a situation when his father was being operated on. His father actually died six times on the operating table when his heart stopped. In spite of that, they were able to resuscitate him back to life.

What kind of verve and vitality for life causes a man to fight so fiercely the throes of death?

I believe because we accept death only as a last resort, we grudgingly put up with it. When death finally comes, we are not really prepared for it. A feeling of emptiness at times is overwhelming. The myriad of emotions that pass through our minds are countless. The anger, bitterness, confusion, fear, anxiety, even guilt roll around in our mind, playing needless head games with us.

A JEWISH WAY OF LIFE

Could it be that we take our negative view of death, that bitter pill that we must swallow, from the Jewish people themselves? In Old Testament times when death occurred, people were not embalmed, and for good reason were buried the next day. I know this is not a common practice in the United States, yet where my ancestors come from in Mexico, it is still practiced today. The Hebrew people would hire professional mourners, who would for the next seven days, mourn a person they never knew. There was quite a ruckus created by a band of folks who were paid handsomely to boisterously sound the alarm that someone had died. If they could create an atmosphere of grief amongst the rest of the family that gathered around in a way that seemed natural, they would have done their job.

The person who died was buried in a simple shroud with no pockets. It was the Jewish belief that all the wealth accumulated during their lifetime could not be taken with them to eternity, hence, no pockets. For those who were still alive and grieving the loss of their loved one, sand was placed in their shoes to make walking somewhat uncomfortable. Mourning a death was not a time to be casually walking through the city. The Jewish people wanted to make sure that they, too, suffered during this time of loss.

It is no wonder then, that in spiritual matters we view death similarly. The resurrection power of the flesh is astounding. It just doesn't want to die. Our carnal nature is so persistent, earnest, purposeful, so determined to make us believe that death to our carnality is a great mistake.

By yielding to the Spirit and dying to our flesh, we are doing nothing more than missing out on all the pleasures, joys, and amusements that life has to offer. On the other hand, the Apostle Paul saw death so much differently, not only physically speaking, but also in the Spirit.

> *Therefore I take pleasure in infirmities, in reproaches, in needs, in persecutions, in distresses, for Christ's sake. For when I am weak, then I am strong.*
>
> (2 Cor 12:10)

He could proclaim this with all audacity because he completely understood where his strength lay. Challenging situations never terrified him, neither did he back away from them because the power and the anointing of God always had him covered. The most demanding conditions, the shipwrecks, the stoning, being bitten by vipers, etc., could not persuade him to change his war cry. What could not be done on his own strength would be accomplished in the power of God's Spirit.

The Lord always knew how to make up the difference when Paul's weakness failed him. Death to the flesh was a daily effort. Paul was cognizant of the fact that if he was to get lazy in spiritual matters, then he too would be overcome by his flesh. His words are somewhat sobering when you consider that he was viewed as the greatest of

85

the apostles, yet he honestly confessed that at his level, he continued to battle his flesh.

A BATTLE THAT IS NEVER CONQUERED

For I know that in me (that is, in my flesh) nothing good dwells; for to will is present with me, but how to perform what is good I do not find. For the good that I will to do, I do not do; but the evil I will not to do, that I practice. Now if I do what I will not to do, it is no longer I who do it, but sin that dwells in me. I find then a law, that evil is present with me, the one who wills to do good.

(Rom 7:18-21)

Now then, it goes without saying that dying to our flesh is paramount to the success of our walk in God. We are going to consider some characteristics of a dead man, both physical and spiritual, that will help us live our lives accordingly.

In the natural, a dead man is oblivious to his surroundings. He is both unaware and unaffected by circumstances, thereby not being able to react to opposing viewpoints. How many times have you seen at a funeral a dead man react to the beautiful young lady who has come to pay her last respects? I've never seen one poke his head out of the casket to admire that sweet thing that has just walked by. Why? He's dead! It's just not possible. You could punch, spit, and even make faces at that same man, and he will not react.

That's just a plain fact; dead men are oblivious to everything that's going on around them.

A MAN ON A MISSION

John the Baptist understood this concept and applied it to his ministry. The man who was chosen to prepare the way for the coming Messiah was completely misunderstood. He was continually mocked for his humble lifestyle, one that included only the bare minimum, as he called the wilderness his home.

Of course, he would never make anyone's 10 best dressed list because his shoddy appearance and camel's hair attire were not considered the fashion of the day. He was laughed to scorn by his choice of cuisine, which boiled down to the ever-yummy locusts and honey.

The fact of the matter was, John was sent by God. He never paid attention to his antagonists for he had a one-track mind. Over and over he would repeat the one and only mission that he was created for: I am...

> *"The voice of one crying in the wilderness: 'Prepare the way of the LORD; Make His paths straight.*
>
> **(Luke 3:4)**

His passion was to fulfill the Scriptures concerning himself, and no one at any time was going to stop him. The effect that death to his flesh and to the world had on his ministry was powerful. The authority in his words made others overlook his funky manner of dress. The impression of those words caused them to search him out in the wilderness. He could not get far enough away from them to stop them from bearing the elements and the dangers of venturing out of the city walls.

They knew where to find him and were willing to pay the price to hear this man of God. When he found himself cooped up in the city jail, he didn't skip a beat; he continued to minister "business as usual." It was at this time, as he was languishing in his jail cell, that he sent his disciples to inquire of Jesus.

They too had heard of a sanctified preacher who had come out of the wilderness, preaching in the power of the Spirit and would like to know if He was the one. Jesus' response to the question was good enough for them:

> *Jesus answered and said to them, "Go and tell John the things you have seen and heard: that the blind see, the lame walk, the lepers are cleansed, the deaf hear, the dead are raised, the poor have the gospel preached to them. And blessed is he who is not offended because of Me."*
>
> (Luke 7:22-23)

WHEN WE FINALLY DIE TO THE FLESH

Our preoccupation with what others think about us has put a damper on our growth. We fuss over our separation from the world, yet it's not the separation that polarizes them from us. It's more the fact that we are too much like them that does not allow them to make the jump over to our side. The real problem is this: we are not completely dead to the flesh or to the world, and we're not fooling anybody.

What will happen when we finally die is this: the power in our words will make others overlook our shortcomings. They will look far and wide to find where we are meeting, insistent on finding out if this church is the true church that they have been looking for. Our response to them will be similar to those that Jesus gave

John's disciples, *"Go your way and tell that the blind see, the lame walk, the lepers are cleansed, the deaf hear, the dead are raised, and to the poor the gospel is preached."* With that manner of anointing flowing freely, we will not be able to contain the masses.

A blind woman walked into a Pentecostal service on Sunday morning. Her hope was that God would miraculously heal her blinded eyes. Little did she know that usually on Sunday mornings, nothing out of the ordinary happened. The preacher that day began to challenge everyone in attendance to believe that for God, nothing was impossible. During the altar call, the blind lady took him at his word and requested him to pray for her so that she could see. Much to the surprise of the preacher, when he did make that prayer of faith that morning, the Lord miraculously healed the blind woman. Of course, the response of the congregation was a positive one, and after the service one by one they congratulated her. Upon nearing the street where they lived, she called out to her husband and made a very strange request.

"Let me drive," said the woman.

Knowing that she did not have a driver's license, he of course responded in shock. He said, "You don't have a license, and furthermore you don't even know how to drive!"

She insisted, "Just let me drive slowly down the street and to enter into our driveway, that's all."

As they switched places and she got behind the wheel, she got real, real happy. As she gently shifted into drive, she cruised down her street like a pro. Honking the horn wildly and frantically waving at anyone who would look her way, she caught the attention of her neighbors. "Isn't that the blind lady who lives down the street?" It sure was the same lady, but she wasn't blind anymore. When the woman finally parked her car, she was surrounded by a horde of people wanting to know what happened.

She said with excitement, "You've got to come with me to the church that I went to this morning. They really do practice what they preach. When he prayed for me, it was so simple. The preacher just said, in the name of Jesus be healed, and my eyes were opened. Boy, I can't wait to get back there next week to see what is going to happen."

Without a doubt, that next Sunday she brought along with her several of her neighbors and filled in pews that the week before were empty. That's what happens when people die to self and allow the Spirit of the Lord to move the way that He would like to.

CHILDLIKE FAITH

The second characteristic of a dead man is his childlike faith. (Refer to Chapter 3 for detail) The boldness of this faith is childlike not childish, one that believes everything. Nothing is out of the question, and when he receives his assignment he doesn't complain, object, dispute, or oppose. He puts his faith into action and lets her rip. This is the type of faith that would be needed when Noah received his instructions to build an ark the size of three football fields. Just building an ordinary ship would be stretching the imagination because Noah was not a shipbuilder by craft. The gathering of the materials for this alone would be a major endeavor, not to mention the fact that he would be building it by himself.

His instructions were to build a boat so big that no one in the history of shipbuilding would ever come close. There was no major body of water anywhere near the construction site, with no one but his small family to occupy this massive ship. He was led to believe that once inside the ark that God would pour down water from Heaven (i.e., rain) enough so that it would allow this oversized vessel to float.

The waters would then continue to rise enough to drown those in the entire world who had not entered into the ark with Noah. If logic was anywhere near the decision making process, it would have shaken him silly to help him come to his senses.

This is the message of doom that Noah had to preach when he wasn't occupying his time building the ark. If there was ever an assignment that sounded cockeyed, it was this one. It would be a hard sell at best. Only a man with childlike faith would have accepted such a challenge without batting an eye. For 120 years he would not waver from the rhema that he had heard. Although he became an embarrassment to all who knew him and even to himself, he died daily and stayed true to his call. He was not going to let adversity be the cause of him turning his back on God.

That's not how Samson would have reacted. Making that kind of sacrifice on a daily basis was not an option in the eyes of this anointed strong man. Living for the moment and loving every minute of it, he lived his life with a reckless abandon. His life was inconsistent and erratic, one that relied on the celestial gifts that were given to him and not on his dedication to God. His prayer life left much to be desired. He turned it on and off when he felt like it, and he was a master of manipulation. Sad to his God was mocked because of his life of radiction.

His miserable end did not justify the means to a life that had dismally gone wrong. At the end of the day, there are more of us who would pattern our lives after Samson than the life of Noah. Like a junkyard dog, we hold on to the fight to the bitter end. Dying is not in our nature, yet if we would cease to fight, the Lord could then take control of our life so we could be blessed beyond measure.

CEASING TO FIGHT

A drowning boy was struggling in the water. His frightened mother stood on the shore and was in agony and grief. By her side stood a strong man, seemingly indifferent to the boy's fate. Again and again the suffering mother appealed to him to save her boy, but he made no move. By and by, the desperate struggles of the boy began to abate. He was losing strength and consequently losing the battle. So weak and helpless, he finally gave up and began to sink. At once the man leaped into the lake and brought the boy in safely to the shore.

"Why did you not save my boy sooner?" asked the now grateful mother.

"Madame, I could not as long as he struggled. He would have dragged us both to certain death. But when he grew weak and ceased to struggle, then it was easy to save him."

It is when we cease from our own works and depend helplessly upon God that we realize how perfectly he is able to save, without any aid from us.

That is the moment when we quit struggling and die to our flesh and the world. We need to take the lead from our Jewish friends. At the time of death, they were covered in simple shrouds without the benefits of any kind of pockets. We would be wise in doing the same. Come into His presence with a pocket-less shroud, one that is void of excuses, fears, and doubts. With no reservations about dying to the flesh, we will then find ourselves in His loving arms, basking in His glory. For this reason and this reason only, God wants us DEAD, NOT ALIVE!

Chapter 7
SENT BY GOD

When He had said these things, He spat on the ground and made clay with the saliva; and He anointed the eyes of the blind man with the clay. And He said to him, "Go, wash in the pool of Siloam" (which is translated, Sent). So he went and washed, and came back seeing.

(John 9:6-7)

When God sends His word, it has to come to pass.

So shall My word be that goes forth from My mouth; It shall not return to Me void, But it shall accomplish what I please, And it shall prosper in the thing for which I sent it.

(Isa 55:11)

Once the word has been given by God, it is our responsibility to receive it (rhema) and unleash it by faith. James in his epistle goes to great lengths to clarify that faith without works is dead (James 2:20). At best, this demonstration of faith is nothing more than hope. Therefore, when we are sent by God, there is an all-embracing confidence in His word. His word to us is the evidence necessary to risk it all, declaring His blessings ahead of time without fearing disapproving repercussions. What is so exciting about this is that the evidence never lies. There is no reason to fear the unknown, to venture out in deep waters, to go where no man has ever gone before; because His word is so dependable, you can take it to the bank.

In His word we find countless promises of blessing, so vast that at times it is unbelievable that the God of the universe would take such good care of us. Yet He does. The psalmist David expounds on this idea in Psalms 103: 2-5

> *Bless the LORD, O my soul, and forget not all His benefits: who forgives all your iniquities, who heals all your diseases, who redeems your life from destruction, who crowns you with loving kindness and tender mercies, who satisfies your mouth with good things, so that your youth is renewed like the eagle's.*

Anyone in their right mind would kill for that kind of benefits package. It is loaded from the get-go. Not only are your sins forgiven, but on top of that any disease or illness that comes your way can be completely restored to health. Not only are you no longer headed to hell in a hand basket, He will daily shower you with kindness and tender mercies. If that's not enough, there is a complete satisfaction in Him.

There is no need for any other; all of our wants and desires are fulfilled in the bosom of our Lord. Finally, our youth is renewed like the eagle's, meaning our life will be long-lived. At the age of 100 the eagle casts all her feathers, being replaced by new ones, so she can be young again.

God through His Spirit recovers us from our decay, and fills us with new life and joy, so that we may return to the days of our youth (Job 33: 25). In that case, responding to the call of God, submitting ourselves to His will is forever a win-win situation.

A BLIND MAN'S FAITH

The blind man Jesus meets in John chapter 9 is a man who has been totally rejected by society. It was common knowledge that everyone believed his blindness was a result of someone sinning in his family, including the disciples. This blind man might as well have been illegitimate because he was always being made fun of and being the butt of all jokes. No one wanted to befriend him because that would talk bad about them. You know how the saying goes; "birds of a feather flock together," don't you? Well, no one wanted to attach themselves to this sinner because that would mean that they, too, would be living in sin. They wanted to make sure that even by mistake; no one could associate them with this offender of the law.

So he lived his life pretty much alone, with not much hope for change because he himself had begun to believe that what the people were saying was true. How could he not believe these lies when he heard them time and time again? His actions spoke louder than words because there was no attempt by him to seek his healing by the pool of

Bethesda (John 5: 1-15). At least the crippled at the poolside had a glimmer of optimism, believing that one day, they too would be healed. That was made evident by their being parked at the pool's edge, waiting for the angel of the Lord to descend from Heaven and trouble the water. The blind man had given up on that idea. As far as he could tell, he was born blind and he was going to die blind, so he might as well come to grips with it and just go out and beg for a living.

Begging alone was the confirmation that the judgment of God had befallen him; he was just accepting his destiny. It is sad to befriend someone who has lost all hope. Their negativity has a way of oozing its way into our psyche, to bring us down to their level so their despair can be shared by all.

It is in this condition that he meets up with Jesus. Before any kinds of miracles are put into place, Jesus first puts everything in order. John records these words in Chapter 9 verse three: ... *"Neither this man nor his parents sinned, but that the works of God should be revealed in him."* In other words, it wasn't important how he got into this situation, but rather that Jesus had the solution. The Lord wanted everybody to know, including the disciples, that there was no sin involved in the blindness of this man. It was necessary to make this point because it was a common belief in those times that all hardships, whether physical, mental, spiritual, or financial, were a result of sin happening somewhere in the family. It is a wonderful lesson to be learned that not all loss is caused by sin.

Too many times, those in despair have been brought to ruin because of the accusing finger that has been pointed at them. Assuming that the trouble that these folks find themselves in has been self-inflicted by the sin in their lives, they are continually badgered into condemnation, and as a result hopelessness sets in. By His words, Jesus wanted to nip this thing in the bud and put it to rest. He would not have it any other way. The priority of this day would be to undo with His word what the words of tradition had destroyed. In hopes that the Lord would resurrect this man's faith, He began to do something very peculiar. He spat on the ground, making clay with the saliva, and He anointed the eyes of the blind man with the clay. What followed was even more bizarre. Jesus commanded him to make his way to the pool of Siloam to wash off the clay and receive his sight.

Let's step back one moment and see what is wrong with this picture. There are too many questions without any answers. The red flags keep popping up and the sirens are blaring. Several things come to mind:

1. How did the blind man know that this homemade concoction of mud would work, understanding that no one was ever healed in this fashion?

2. Why was Jesus sending him to the pool of Siloam when it was at the pool of Bethesda that the crippled were healed?

3. How in the world was he supposed to get there? Not only was he blind, but Jesus did not give him any directions.

4. Would it do any good to be sent on the Sabbath? The Sabbath was meant as a day of rest.

5.

SILOAM MEANS SENT

The significance of the order lay in the word "Siloam." Siloam means sent. If you are being sent by God, with your specific rhema in hand, you could be sent to the wrong place, on the wrong day, without any directions, doing it the wrong way, and still be successful. Why, because you have been sent by God. His commissioning of your life will override any and all laws that have been set up to abide by. Being sent by Him makes all the difference in the world, such that you can withstand the barrage of scoffers and mockers that will come out of the woodwork to put your faith to the test.

"Hey, blind man, where are you going with that mud plastered on your eyes?"

"I'm trying to locate the pool of Siloam."

"What in the world are you going to do when you get there, you crazy old man?"

"I'm going to get healed."

"Hey knucklehead, you're going in the wrong direction to the wrong pool. Who told you to do this, anyway?"

"Jesus did the son of God."

"Son of a what? There ain't no God here telling you nothing. It's probably some crackpot taking advantage of you because you're blind. Come on, man, wise up. It's the Sabbath, for crying out loud. There is nothing miraculous that's going to happen to you today, don't you know the law?"

"It may be as you say, but the son of God sent me and today I am receiving my sight."

For all the ridicule that this blind man had to undergo, his obedience to the word of God (his rhema) was enough to recover his eyesight. I think the blind man's greatest contribution to this miracle was the unleashing of his faith. What person in his right mind would allow a perfect stranger to put mud made from saliva on his eyes, knowing that the backlash of this act would stir up the pot of criticism? It was bad enough that he was already the laughingstock of Jerusalem, how much more would he have to take? When God sends His word, He understands that most will not accept it because of its foolishness in nature.

> But God has chosen the foolish things of the world to put to shame the wise, and God has chosen the weak things of the world to put to shame the things which are mighty; and the base things of the world and the things which are despised God has chosen, and the things which are not, to bring to nothing the things that are, that no flesh should glory in His presence.
>
> (1 Cor 1:27-29)

You can never second-guess the choices that God makes. Once He makes up His mind to call out someone to accomplish His will, whether He is considered weak or base, He will never renege on that choice. That person may be the most despised on the face of the earth, and that needn't matter because wherever he is lacking, God's grace is sufficient to make up the difference.

AMAZING RESULTS
For all that this blind man wasn't, the Lord still believed that this chosen vessel would become a vessel of

honor with all of the glory going to God. Look at the results of the unleashing of his faith. When he finally found his way to the pool of Siloam and washed the mud from his eyes as instructed, the miracle he longed for gloriously unfolded just the way Jesus said it would. But wait! It was even more glorious than what he could have ever imagined. Upon receiving his sight, there was no need to adjust his eyes to the light. That's unheard of. How many times have you gone into your teenagers' darkened room about noontime, only to find that he is still asleep? Any red-blooded American mother knows how to remedy that situation, by opening the room-darkening blinds, of course.

Upon entering the room, the light blinds him to the point that one hears shrieks of, "Mom, stop it." The light is too much for his eyes, blinding him momentarily until he has the opportunity to slowly focus. Well, that just didn't happen to the blind man. He was seeing for the first time ever in his life, yet in spite of this he went about his business as if he had been able to see from day one. The transition from being blind to a world that fancied all of the colors of the rainbow was a smooth one. Although everything was new, in reality nothing was new because of the perfection of this answered prayer.

The unleashing of our faith can bring similar results, ones that are just as amazing. The Lord has the ability to erase your hurts, losses, anxieties, and all of the bad memories from the past as if they had never happened in the first place. This is possible even when you are at fault. Once you are chosen then sent, God will take care of the rest.

UNLEASHING HER FAITH

I ministered to a pregnant young lady as I was visiting her church for the first time. At the moment that I called her out from her seat into the aisle, I could see that she was very nervous. I began to inquire of the Lord the reason for so much of her anxiety. He said that she was overly concerned for the health of her baby because she was afraid that as a judgment from God, the baby was going to be born deformed.

Even though the Lord had forgiven her of her past indiscretion, Satan continued to play mind games and was winning. Because this was a delicate situation, I decided to give her the message God had given to me in her ear. I more or less said this, that not only did God forgive her and place it under the blood; she would also give birth to a normal baby without any birth defects.

I abruptly stopped this message and took a couple of steps back. A spirit of boldness fell upon me and I began to survey the congregation. With a voice of warning, I pointed my finger to them and said, "For those of you who have judged and condemned this young lady with the severity and harshness that you have, watch out! If you continue this injustice, the judgment that you wish upon her will fall upon you." I then prayed for her that God would give her the wherewithal to keep on going. I sensed a peace come over her and she then sat down.

A couple weeks later, I found out that this young lady was in truth the Pastor's daughter. It was an uphill battle for her until the baby was born, but God's grace was sufficient for her. I remember her telling me that while in labor, the Lord brought to her memory that day, my words, and His promise. It was enough to give birth to a beautiful little girl, all for the honor and glory of God. As I have looked at her minister on the platform, subsequent to that time as one of the praise singers, I could not help but think that the Lord had erased all of the hurts of her past. This is something that God is willing to do if we, too, will put our faith to work.

As we wind down this chapter, re-examining the faith of this un-expecting blind man, the thing that cannot be overlooked about this incredible miracle was the fact that the Lord did it while passing by. Healing a blind man wasn't necessarily a scheduled part of His day, per se, but as the opportunity presented itself, the Lord was more than willing to oblige. God took the time to first of all choose this blind man and all of his inadequacies. He then sent him with His word, which was good enough to produce a miracle. It is simply mind-boggling what the Lord can do at a whim. You can use any adjective and it would fit. Our God is simply unbelievable, incredible, inconceivable, beyond belief, staggering, mind-blowing, fantastic, remarkable, and so on and so on and so on! Need I say more? Well, I will. He not only provides for us unreservedly, He does it in perfection without any side effects, with willingness beyond measure.

If we honestly believe that we have been sent by God, then and only then will His word come to pass.

MOVING MY FAMILY TO TEXAS

Last year in March of 2009, my wife and I made the decision to move our family to the state of Texas. Both of us had lived our entire lives in California, and making the move to the Lone Star State was a colossal one. Our roots had been established so deeply that moving from California was like severing your right arm. All of our family and friends were in California. The business contacts my wife had made in real estate were in California. We lived in Southern California in an area that was unquestionably ideal. We were centrally localized to all of the wonderful attractions the Golden State had to offer. Dodger Stadium was about 40 minutes away, as was the Memorial Coliseum, the stadium that housed the USC Trojans.

The Staples Center, the home of the world champion Los Angeles Lakers was freeway close, not to mention The Pantry Restaurant, just the few blocks away, where you can buy the best breakfast in the world, 24 hours a day. Don't get me started on all the good places you could eat, because I would be here all day. You could hightail it to the beach in less than an hour, and the snowcapped mountains of Big Bear could be had in a two-hour drive. If you wanted to be daring, a three-hour drive would take you to the friendly borders of Mexico, where shopping was always an adventure. Anything and everything that life could offer was available to us and in abundance.

So then, when the call of God came, stating that Texas was to be our next home, there was quite some apprehension. There were mitigating circumstances that made this decision a little bit easier, but the bottom line was that it was going to be very, very hard to leave. If it were not for the fact that my ministry had been slowly but surely closing in California, I would have never given it a second thought. As hard as I tried to make things work, Pastors were leery of any signs and wonders ministry that they could not figure out.

On top of that, real estate sales had taken a complete dive and there was no income coming from my wife. She too was utterly frustrated by the new rules that were making securing a loan nearly impossible.

That being said, the only thing that I could latch onto and have confidence in was knowing I was being sent by God.

When we arrived in Texas, there was no family or friends to greet us. There were no familiar surroundings to pacify us. Everything was new and scary, but I had been sent by God. A year has now passed, and proclaiming that the decision to move was the greatest thing that could ever happen to us is an understatement. I have been introduced to people of influence, who have helped open the doors to a ministry that in California had almost died. I have now started to travel internationally, both to Central and South America.

My anointing has become deeper, so much so that I cannot recall from the past a move of God so powerful in me. My ministry caters to the smaller church and those with 100 members or less. Well, from March 2009 to February 2010, the Lord has filled 1,127 people with the baptism of the Holy Ghost and has healed 905. The healings have included people who were blind, deaf, and paralytic, coupled with those who suffered diseases, such as cancer, fibromyalgia, arthritis, diabetes, high blood pressure, and the like.

This sovereign move of God could only be the confirmation that I had been sent by God. His word was enough to catapult me to a place in Him that I had never been before. The scary thing about this is the fact that it continues to grow and the sky appears to be the limit. I remember now a prophecy that I received in California right before we made this move. The young man, who was prophesying, in my mind, was just showing off. He wanted to let me know that his ministry was just as powerful as mine, so what he had to say kind of fell on deaf ears. His words were to the effect that my ministry was about to move in a new dimension, one that included signs and wonders that would be unleashed in far-off lands. As I ponder the direction that God is taking me in this new year, I realize that those words are coming closer and closer to becoming a reality. This was made possible because I was sent by God.

> *So shall My word be that goes forth from My mouth; It shall not return to Me void, But it shall accomplish what I please, And it shall prosper in the thing for which I sent it.*
>
> (Isa 55:11)

I have been sent by God, have you?

Chapter 8
PARADOXES

*For whoever desires to save his life will lose it,
but whoever loses his life for My sake and the
gospel's will save it*

(Mark 8:35)

A life of faith is full of paradoxes. To save your life in
God you must lose it, and the way up is down. To rule in
the kingdom of God, you must be willing to serve, and to
be considered the first amongst the brethren you must be
last. It is a life that has neither rhyme nor reason.
Certainly it is a life that can never be figured out. I think
to better understand what a paradox is, it is prudent that
we put a handle on it and define it for clarity. According
to **Webster's Dictionary**, a paradox is a statement that is
seemingly contradictory. It is expressed in a manner
opposite to what is logical or expected.

The definition includes being opposed to common
sense and yet is perhaps true. If there were ever a situation
where the definition of paradox applies, it is certainly true
in the life of a Christian.

Paradoxes are essential to hearing the voice of God. Logic and reasoning cause the static that makes God's instructions to us unclear. Lack of clarity triggers doubt, and doubt unbelief.

> *Beware, brethren, lest there be in any of you an evil heart of unbelief in departing from the living God; but exhort one another daily, while it is called "Today," lest any of you be hardened through the deceitfulness of sin. ...while it is said: "Today, if you will hear His voice, Do not harden your hearts as in the rebellion."*
>
> (Heb 3:12-13, 15)

ISRAEL WANDERS AIMLESSLY

Unbelief is the result of a hardened heart. It is exactly what happened to Israel as they wandered aimlessly in the desert. Living for God by faith was too much of a stretch for them and the mystery of faith was never embraced. They were constantly offended by Moses' leadership, and their disapproval turned into disagreement and disagreement into unbelief. Their hardened hearts of unbelief would not permit them entrance into the Promised Land.

> *So we see that they could not enter in because of unbelief.*
>
> (Heb 3:19)

To tell you the truth, Moses was only one step ahead of this backslidden bunch. He, too, was just as inept as they were in understanding this concept, because living by faith was foreign to him as well. As the call of God came to him again at age 80, the Lord found him tending sheep in the desert. His résumé now included running away from his initial call as he fled Egypt, being branded a murderer and coward. Two-thirds of his life, he was spiritually apart from the will of God. His mental state didn't do him any favors. Why? He had lost out 40 years ago on leading Israel out of Egypt, and in his mind it was too late in his life for a do-over. I'm sure that thoughts now drifted more towards retirement than leading a nation out of captivity.

His burning bush experience began to speak volumes in his life, for it too was a paradox of sorts. This bush that he stumbled upon continued to burn and burn and burn, and yet it was not consumed. He began to believe that this was a God thing, and although God had been somewhat silent to him within the past 40 years, something was up. There really was no logical explanation, it had to be God. As he approached the bush and God began to speak to him personally, it allowed him to release his faith. With this newfound assurance, he could now believe God for this new call that would appear preposterous in the eyes of others.

> *For the gifts and the calling of God are irrevocable.*
>
> (Rom 11:29)

The call of God is irrevocable, it will never expire and cannot be canceled, disregarded, go unnoticed or overlooked. We have been destined for greatness and that cannot be undone. It doesn't matter who has told you any different. The word of God is our evidence, one that does not lie, and we can be completely confident that God will always have our back no matter what anybody says. When our ministry and/or character are put to the test, being tried in the fire, they will burn brighter and hotter yet not consumed, and God will get all the glory.

THE PARADOXES CONTINUE IN MOSES' LIFE

Moses was now ready to proceed to a new level of paradoxes. He was given orders to lead Israel out of captivity with nothing but failure written all over them. God warned him ahead of time that Pharaoh would not respond to the voice of God; nevertheless he must experience this embarrassment regardless. Moses obeyed God's orders to a tee, yet to no avail. Perhaps Moses believed that when God unleashed His glory, that that in and of itself would soften the heart of Pharaoh. The signs and wonders that the Lord would display surely would convince Pharaoh that Jehovah was the God of the universe and His people must be let go to worship this all powerful God.

To his dismay, it only made matters worse, Pharaoh hardened his heart even more so, and Moses looked like a fool. Not once, not twice, but nine times. It wasn't until Pharaoh lost his son that he finally came to his senses and allowed Moses to lead God's people out of Egypt.

If you have lived in God long enough, something similar to this will happen to you. You will know ahead of time that your assignment is going to fail, you will be made the laughingstock of all those involved, and the definition of "fool" will unquestionably apply.

We are fools for Christ's sake, but you are wise in Christ! We are weak, but you are strong! You are distinguished, but we are dishonored! To the present hour we both hunger and thirst, and we are poorly clothed, and beaten, and homeless. And we labor, working with our own hands. Being reviled, we bless; being persecuted, we endure; being defamed, we entreat. We have been made as the filth of the world, the offscouring of all things until now.

(1 Cor 4:10-13)

We are fools for Christ's sake. Like Moses, we are hung out to dry. Our folly is exposed to the entire world and we are laughed at. Without a leg to stand on, not being able to defend ourselves, we walk away totally devastated and embarrassed.

AN UTTER EMBARRASSMENT

For approximately 10 years, I had preached throughout the United States about a testimony that never came to pass. This powerful testimony happened during the initial stages of my training in signs and wonders. I remember those years I was so afraid to step out by faith that I was very cautious not to go out on a limb. Because the Lord knew that I was pretty much satisfied in taking baby steps regarding faith, with His instructions usually came quite a few confirmations to let me feel comfortable in doing what He asked. This situation involved a woman (the youth director's wife) who could not get pregnant in over 10 years of marriage. As I arrived at the weekend youth camp I was invited to, I was overly excited because just the week before I had received a special anointing from God. It's somewhat hard to explain other than the fact that when this type of anointing falls upon me, God does extraordinary things. This special anointing fell upon me once again when greeting the director's wife on the second day of camp. It was so strong and powerful that it scared me half to death and brought great fear immediately to my life. I went back to my cabin and began to pray for help. I had never laid hands on a person in this type of condition, didn't know what to do, or how to go about it. For what seemed like an eternity in prayer, God continued to assure me that if I trusted Him, He would do it.

As time came to minister later in the evening, I called her up. With a word of knowledge, I assured her that God was going to give her a baby girl when she and her husband left their position as district directors. This was a confirmation of a word given to her just two weeks prior to the camp, and it was enough to believe God for the impossible. The prophecy became even more incredible when I approached her husband after the service. When he mentioned to me an even greater confirmation, I was completely blown away by his words. He said that if after the prayer that was made that night we began to count the days that were left in his term, there were exactly nine months left. In other words, God was going to bless him and his wife with a baby girl in nine months. The problem is that the baby was never born.

Adding insult to injury, talking to this man of God about the incident later, he did not recall any of the specifics of that weekend. In his recollection, none of the things that I remember were ever a part of the promise. The timing was off, there was no other prophecy two weeks prior, and of course the baby was never born. I did everything right and it still came out wrong. I came out of the situation looking like a fool, totally humiliated. In the past I have heard men of God say things behind a pulpit that were highly exaggerated, but as I look back on this experience, it was way too specific, with too many confirmations to be made up. To this day, I cannot explain it, but neither will I make excuses to make myself look good. I must file this experience in the "I just don't know what happened" file.

For now we see in a mirror, dimly, but then face to face. Now I know in part, but then I shall know just as I also am known.

(1 Cor 13:12)

There are a lot of things that happen in God that I do not understand and perhaps never will. Yet there is one lesson that I learned from early on in my ministry. It is something that many men are not comfortable with; nevertheless it is something that I constantly do. If I do not know an answer to a question that is proposed to me, I will flat-out admit it. If I'm given the chance to research the question to find an answer, then I will do my very best to do so. If not, I will not make up something just to make myself look good.

MOSES' SADDEST OF PARADOXES

Returning to the life of Moses, there was a paradox in his life that cannot be construed other than the word sad. He was not permitted to enter into the Promised Land. It appeared that he had been grouped into the same rebellious bunch that could not enter in either. For all of his efforts at leading Israel out of Egypt, this judgment of God makes no sense at all. What about the intense face-to-face encounters with Pharaoh? Or the lack of confidence Israel showed in him, although God performed signs and wonders every step of the way? We can't leave out the day-to-day rebellion that led to the thoughts of leaving this responsibility in someone else's hands. Finally, he had to battle daily the self-doubt of his own leadership abilities, because these people complained no matter what.

For one act of disobedience, God prohibited him entering into that blessed rest. Looking back on his life, it looks as if all of the good he had done had been undone. This judgment appears overly harsh when considering that God forgave Israel time and time again. It would seem so reasonable that God would cut Moses a little bit of slack, but this is the paradox that is the most confusing, one that we will never quite understand.

Although not entering into the Promised Land appears to knock Moses off the pedestal of the great leaders in Israel, there is one last paradox that I would like to consider in his life that will help us understand why he is held in such high esteem today, even when his life ended in failure. It is a paradox somewhat hidden in the Old Testament, yet powerful in its application.

A POWERFUL PARADOX HIDDEN TO MOST

We must go back to his second call to lead Israel out of Egypt into the Promised Land. His call to become the Hebrew Messiah, so to speak, should have never transpired in the first place.

It had nothing to do with his advanced age or his unfaithfulness to his first call. Buried amongst the myriad of rules, regulations, and requirements that define the office of a Hebrew priest is a particular one that disqualifies Moses from the get-go.

And the LORD spoke to Moses, saying, "Speak to Aaron, saying: 'No man of your descendants in succeeding generations, who has any defect, may approach to offer the bread of his God. For any man who has a defect shall not approach: a man blind or lame, who has a marred face or any limb too long, a man who has a broken foot or broken hand, or is a hunchback or a dwarf, or a man who has a defect in his eye, or eczema or scab, or is a eunuch. No man of the descendants of Aaron the priest, who has a defect, shall come near to offer the offerings made by fire to the LORD. He has a defect; he shall not come near to offer the bread of his God. He may eat the bread of his God, both the most holy and the holy; only he shall not go near the veil or approach the altar, because he has a defect, lest he profane My sanctuaries; for I the LORD sanctify them."

(Lev 21:16-23)

This law states that in order to become eligible as a practicing priest, not only would he have to be a descendent from the tribe of Levi, but physically he could not have any defect whatsoever. That being said, the speech impediment that indeed hindered Moses' communication skills would be the defect that would prohibit him offering sacrifices, but even more important, deny him access to the presence of God found beyond the veil in the temple.

One might argue that this is a moot point because Moses was a prophet, not a priest. However, in His foreknowledge, the Lord made His call to Moses as a prophet before the law could disqualify him as a priest. This was where one of the most powerful paradoxes in Moses life began to unfold.

The Lord actually went to the future to pull grace from that generation, bringing it back to the time of the Exodus so that Moses could receive this sovereign call of God without breaking any rules. Although he could never qualify as a priest, a higher calling awaited, allowing him the opportunity of a lifetime that would have been impossible under the law.

He went on to such greatness that even his failed ending could not put a damper on how he would be perceived in the generations to come. How does Moses' life personally affect us in our daily walk with God? It helps us to understand just how far God is willing to go to use anyone in His kingdom.

This slow-tongued, fearful man, who impressed no one with his people skills, was still able to catch the attention of the Master, to be chosen for one of the greatest assignments that will go down in the history of the Hebrew people.

God was willing to use an ordinary man who stuttered to accomplish remarkable feats that would prove once and for all that Jehovah God was the one and only God of the universe.

I TOO SHOULD HAVE BEEN DISQUALIFIED

I, for my part, hold a great admiration for this meek man of God because I, too, am somewhat of a paradox in Pentecostal circles, in more ways than one. I had written in a prior chapter that the Lord had given me a promise to heal my weakened right leg. Several years have now passed, and although I have been obedient to His instructions to receive my healing, my waiting on Him continues.

This is where the paradox begins as I attempt to run on the ever-shrinking leg. The longer I run, the stronger the leg gets, which baffles the doctors to no end. According to their knowledge and past experiences, the leg should be getting weaker, not stronger. For the period of time that I choose to exercise, there comes a time in my effort that God allows the leg to function as normal, which cannot be backed up medically.

I, too, do not have an answer for this medical marvel, other than the fact that because jogging is important to me, it has become important to Him. What makes this move of God even more bizarre is that when I am done with my exercising, the leg goes back to its weakened form and I struggle to walk normally. Go figure.

That doesn't even scratch the surface in the world of the peculiar, because receiving a call from God that includes a miraculous healing ministry in most eyes would appear ludicrous. How could a man crippled from polio have the audacity to lay hands on the sick, believing that God would heal them when God has yet to respond to his own needs? My right hand that was affected by this childhood disease is weak, frail, fragile, feeble and at times lifeless. Nevertheless, under the anointing in the name of Jesus, it becomes a powerful instrument of healing. I am totally aware of the fact that if I were to have lived in Old Testament times, my physical disability would have disallowed me the wonderful relationship that I now have with my heavenly Father. If it were not for His grace, I too would be limited to view His majesty from afar. I would only be able to hear about Him, but never have the opportunity to know Him. For this I will forever be grateful for God's grace.

> *For by grace you have been saved through faith, and that not of yourselves; it is the gift of God, not of works, lest anyone should boast.*
> (Eph 2:8-9)

Grace truly is the paradox of all paradoxes, one which gives us total access to the throne of God, and undeservedly so. We needn't worry about measuring up anymore, because the grace that was demonstrated on Calvary was enough to bring into our lives reconciliation to God. It is genuinely a gift that keeps on giving, one for which we will be forever grateful.

Chapter 9
WHEN THE BOWL
IS FULL

Now to Him who is able to do exceedingly
abundantly above all that we ask or think,
according to the power that works in us,

(Eph 3:20)

God is not directly in control of everything. That is
somewhat of a shocking statement, wouldn't you say? We
have always been taught that God is in control, that the
Master of the universe has everything under wraps, and
we needn't worry about a thing because nothing ever
happens unless He permits it. It sounds so right, so the way
it's supposed to be, but then why are there unexplainable
disasters that leave families torn apart? If God is in
complete control, why are young ladies being raped or
sexually abused by loved ones? There are millions in this
world dying of hunger, including innocent little ones who
have nothing to eat. Would a God in control allow this
needless suffering? Daily we put up with unsolved

murders, racial unrest, overpopulation, drug cartels and the like.

Yet we go on our merry little way, believing that all that is not right in the world falls into the category of the perfect will of God. We heartily quote the promises of God, those that protect us, provide for us, and heal us, defending the position that for our God there is nothing impossible. The fact of the matter is this: the promises of God are not automatic, but rather conditional. That means if we do our part, then God will do His. There is a responsibility that has been placed upon us to participate in the blessings that God has planned for us, and it is the key in seeing the mighty hand of God move in our lives. Sad to say, when we don't, it opens the door to bitterness, which then yields to unbelief.

WHAT EASILY OFFENDS US

We are so easily offended when we are told that our unbelief has kept us from receiving from God, yet Scripture tells us that if we believe and do not doubt, we will receive (Matt.17:20, Mk 11:22). When we are told that our inability to hold on has created the lack in our life, the offense continues, even though the Scriptures tell us through faith and patience we inherit our promises (Heb. 6:12). When we have not moved on a situation and it has caused failure, it irks us because Scripture points an accusing finger our way, saying that if we would have been willing and obedient, we would have eaten of the good of the land (Isa. 1:19).

Curses that come to our lives because of a lack of tithing do not sit well with us, although the Scripture is quite clear in this light (Mal. 3:8-12). We don't forgive, and still expect God to hear our prayers and answer them

(Mk 11: 25, 26). We eat poorly, don't exercise, abuse our bodies and we blame our sickness on being God's will. We don't properly train our children, and are offended when their rebellion could be our fault (Deut. 6:7, Pro. 22: 6). The list goes on and on and on.

What we have failed to consider is that we have been made laborers together with Him (2 Cor. 6:1). We have a special invitation to participate in the splendor of Heaven because God has decided not to make this a one-man show. He moves according to the power in us, which should excite us to no end. Why? Because the power that moves in us is nothing more than the *dunamis (miraculous power)* of the Holy Ghost. Now, I am going to state something that will have both a positive and negative reaction. *When you received the gift of the Holy Ghost, you received all the power that you will ever receive.*

For those of you who truly understand that statement, you are probably doing cartwheels about now. For those of you who don't understand what I mean, believing that the power that you now possess could not save you from an attack from the enemy even if your life depended up upon it, give me some time to explain. The problem is not that you have not received enough power to overcome life's daily adversities; the problem lies in not releasing the power that you have been given. I will go into greater detail about releasing that power in a bit. However, let me backtrack and help you understand that God's power is measurable. Just like faith, grace, and love, there are levels that can be measured.

JESUS AT HIS WORST
When Jesus decided to make a stop in Nazareth, the city that He was raised in, He was not received with open

arms, as He had been in the other cities that He had visited (Mark 6:5). Because the people who had known Him all of His life could not accept that He was the self-proclaimed Messiah, He could not perform any miracles. This lack of power had nothing to do with Him, more so with the fact that the people would not release their faith to let the power of God move. It was this unbelief that short-circuited the power line from Heaven, and in turn forfeited the blessings that other cities were receiving. It was so true when Jesus made this statement:

> *For Jesus Himself testified that a prophet has no honor in his own country.*
> **(John 4:44)**

I have been able to learn this lesson firsthand. The signs and wonders ministry that God has given to me is one that has unfolded over a long period of time. For years and years, without any kind of demonstrative show of God's power, I poked along without much fanfare. Once God began to move miraculously in my ministry, it appeared to have happened overnight. Cancers were being healed, blinded eyes were being opened, deaf ears were being unstopped in a short period of time, and to be quite truthful, it was overwhelming. Of course, the greatest criticism came from my local church. For years and years they had known this quiet man, standing behind a pulpit with nothing more than heartfelt, tear-filled messages. Lo and behold, when news got out what was happening at the other churches that I had ministered in, they thought the others were talking about someone else. Sure enough, when I came to minister in our own local church, not much happened. That was enough to prove to them that what they had heard was nothing more than a ruse.

The disapproving, nitpicking, judgmental eyes that were riveted on me would be enough to discredit the Lord Jesus Christ Himself. I have gleaned such great lessons from this experience, ones that have helped as I go to churches that are similarly non-responsive. I remember on one occasion when the Lord would continue to allow me to return to a particular church, one that was totally indifferent to the move of God.

I asked Him irritably, "Why do you continue to bring me back to this place when nobody responds to my ministry?"

"For the offering, of course," He answered. "Offering? You know that I don't work that way."

"Perhaps, but you have to understand that they don't listen to me either!"

WHEN GREAT POWER IS IN EFFECT

On the other side of the spectrum, the power demonstrated in the life of Peter and John appeared immeasurable (Acts 4:33). After an intense time of consecration, 50 days of prayer and fasting in the upper room where the Holy Ghost fell for the first time, they made their way to the temple to pray. As they came across a lame man begging at the temple gate, the beggar asked alms of them. In his surprise, the beggar was not sure how to respond to Peter's answer, which was, "Silver and gold have I none, but such as I have give I onto you." Before the beggar had any time to make sense of Peter's words, Peter grabbed him by the hand and declared, "In the name of Jesus Christ, rise up and walk." The Scriptures say that immediately his feet and ankle bones received strength and he went away walking, leaping, and praising God.

Why was there such a disparate show of power? What we see in Nazareth and what happened at the temple appear to go from one extreme to the other. The difference is found not only in the measure of power that had been unleashed that ultimately determines how great the miracle will be, but the response to that power as well. This beggar was hungry for more than what money could buy. And when the opportunity presented itself, he took full advantage of the power that was being unleashed by these humble men of God.

Persevering is vital in the releasing of God's power. A single prayer of despair will not move Heaven to the point that we will receive what is being asked. Consider the perseverance of Elijah. He was put in a situation where a widow woman came to him with a precarious request. Her son had died and she was asking the prophet to raise him from the dead. He prayed for the child to no avail. With a second attempt to pacify the widow, he also came up empty. Not until he prayed the third time was the child resurrected.

Why did it take three prayers? Why couldn't this miracle transpire after one prayer? Was he not spiritually ready, or was there not enough faith? Could it be that he prayed wrong the first two times, and it wasn't until the third prayer that God understood the request? The answer to all of these questions lies in the fact that every time Elijah prayed, he was releasing more and more and more power from the throne of God. His persevering requests were enough to release the sufficient amount of power to finally raise this child from the dead.

RAISING THE DEAD IN TODAY'S WORLD

How many prayers are needed in order to raise someone from the dead? I really couldn't answer that question with a definite number. Listen to this testimony that I heard several years ago. A young evangelist had been summoned to a hospital where a particular person was gravely ill. He did the best that he could to minister to that person before he actually prayed. With all the faith that he could muster, he prayed that God would heal that person miraculously. Unfortunately, the person died. Feeling somewhat of a failure, he thought about calling the nurses and to unceremoniously disappear.

What he heard next from Heaven threw him for a loop, for God was requesting him to continue praying until He resurrected that person from the dead. Somewhat rattled by the request, he awkwardly began to pray. A short while later, he got into the Spirit and began to speak in tongues.

The noise caused a ruckus in the corridors of the hospital, and immediately a nurse walked in to see what was going on. Noticing that the patient had died, she was somewhat dumbfounded by what the young evangelist was doing. She asked him if he realized that the patient had died, and to this he replied, yes, and continued on.

He continued to become more boisterous about the time he had been praying for about 15 minutes. Another nurse hurried into the room to settle him down, but to no avail. He continued deeper in the Spirit, where tears coupled with moaning and groaning overwhelmed him; he had been praying now for about 20 minutes. His prayers continued into deep travail, and at this point the head nurse walked into the room and asked him to leave.

When he didn't respond to her pleas, she walked out of the room to call the hospital police, and when she returned after he had been going at it for 30 minutes, the police prepared to escort him out of the room. At this time, the person was raised from the dead, to the amazement of all.

This young man understood a concept that few of us have been able to grasp. If we will obey the voice of God and complete our assignment, unleashing His power through prayer, somewhere down the line God will come through and answer our appeal.

WHY THE POWER SHORTAGE?

The question then must be asked, if releasing the power of God through prayer is the answer, then why is there such a great power shortage? The power source, in all truth, is not the problem. It's an operator problem. The power that is being released through us doesn't even tip the scales. This is what Strong says about Ephesians 3:20. "God is going to do it super abundantly more than we can ask or think in the measure of the power that is *distributed* from us." There has to be a constant distributing of His power through prayer. Praying every once in awhile just won't cut it.

> *The effective, fervent prayer of a righteous man avails much.*
>
> (James 5:16)

Wuest's Dictionary says of this Scripture, "a prayer of a righteous person is able to do much as it operates." The Amplified Version of the Bible says the earnest (heartfelt, continued) prayer of a righteous man makes tremendous power available (dynamic in its working). Is it any wonder why Satan fights so hard to keep us from our knees? I believe that he understands this concept better than we do ourselves, and goes the extra mile to make sure that we do not wake up to the knowledge that there is an abundance of power in us that just needs to be released. Every prayer counts, and the more we pray the earnest, heartfelt, continued prayer, the more dynamic we will become in releasing God's power from above.

What is most discouraging about prayer, in my view, is the fact that we really don't know if our prayers are being effective enough to get a response from God. Am I praying enough? Am I saying the right words? Does He even know that I am alive?

Why bother with something that is so mysterious that we have no guarantees of success? These are the same questions that I had brooded over for years when I came upon the Scriptures that I will share with you today. There is an actual process that goes on in Heaven that takes most of the mystery out of our prayer life. This process, of course, still includes faith, so just to let you know it's not a get rich quick scheme.

Now when He had taken the scroll, the four living creatures and the twenty-four elders fell down before the Lamb, each having a harp, and golden bowls full of incense, which are the prayers of the saints.

(Rev 5:8)

PRAYER BOWLS

The prayers of the saints, you and I, are put in individual bowls. As we begin to bring our petitions before the Lord in prayer, they are converted into the incense, and then placed in one of these bowls until they are filled. What happens next is just fascinating.

> *Then another angel, having a golden censer, came and stood at the altar. He was given much incense, that he should offer it with the prayers of all the saints upon the golden altar which was before the throne. And the smoke of the incense, with the prayers of the saints, ascended before God from the angel's hand. Then the angel took the censer, filled it with fire from the altar, and threw it to the earth. And there were noises, thunderings, lightnings, and an earthquake.*
>
> (Rev 8:3-5)

This other angel that the Scripture talks about is none other than the Lord Jesus Christ Himself in His priestly role, having with Him His golden censer. When enough prayer has been accumulated and that prayer bowl is full, it is then offered upon the golden altar. This is where things get really exciting. When the smoke of the incense ascends up before God, the censer is taken and filled with fire from the altar and cast down unto the earth. Something awesome happens in the Spirit that then begins to affect the natural realm.

The thundering, lightning and earthquakes are nothing more than our reaction to the massive blessing that we have just received.

Let me put it this way. We are completely blown away by the gaudy, demonstrative, fashion with which God expresses Himself. Because we don't really know when our prayer bowl will be filled, His provision strikes quickly like thunder and lightening and its impact is so great it shakes us to the core of our foundation. But truth be told, it really isn't a miracle, because we have paid a great price in prayer to receive what we have received. This is where faith comes into the picture.

It is by faith we continue to pray, even when it looks as if nothing is happening in Heaven. We continue to pray even when standing on His promise will bring a backlash of scoffers and mockers to make us second-guess our strength of will.

In praying for the sick, far too much attention is paid to those who are terminally ill. Human nature is such that we don't perk up in church until a situation arises where a miracle is needed. Because a miracle is not an everyday occurrence, the jury is out on a man performing until something happens that is undoubtedly considered a God thing. The healing of headaches, backaches, and toothaches aren't enough to pacify these miracle seekers, so they always cry out for more.

BEING PUT ON THE SPOT

You could feel the change in the atmosphere of the congregation when a blind man slowly made his way to the altar. With his sunglasses hiding his disability, he did not appear to be blind. I asked him to take off the sunglasses, to better assess the situation. Sure enough, he was completely blind. I proceeded to ask him to do something that not only would be difficult to complete, but also show me where his faith was.

I asked him if he would be willing to walk up and down the aisle by himself to receive his healing. He responded affirmatively and began his little excursion down the aisle without any help. He clumsily bumped into the pews; almost falling down, but unscathed continued to walk. It took quite a while for him to complete his journey, and when he returned there was no change in his condition. You could hear an all-embracing sigh from the congregation, making known their disappointment. I asked him to do it again, and without a hitch he started anew.

When he returned, the result was the same. I asked him to do it one more time, and undaunted in his faith he went again. This time the right eye began to see somewhat blurry, and there was some hope. I asked him to repeat the process four more times, seven times in all. At the end of his effort, there still was no change in either eye. Even though there was not a significant change in his eyesight, I sensed in my spirit that I was releasing more and more and more power as I went along. I told him to continue to walk daily without the use of a cane or a walker or human help. He agreed, and we left it at that. I called the Pastor the next week for an update and he was happy to announce that the young man was baptized both in water and in Spirit that Sunday.

I returned to the church about three months later, looking for him, and he was nowhere to be found. After the service was over, a young man who I did not recognize came to the platform to greet me. He asked me if I had remembered him, a question that is forever asked me. When he saw a puzzled look on my face, he said, "I'm the blind guy, don't you remember?" He was wearing glasses to help the left eye see better. The right eye was completely normal, and from the last time I had seen him, the Lord opened the left eye. I had admonished him to continue praying so that the Lord could finish the work, and of course he agreed. Three months subsequent to that, I happened to call his Pastor for another matter and he asked me if I remembered the blind man. Of course I did. How could I forget? He went on to say that that day, the blind man had actually gotten his driver's license and that he was completely healed.

Praying and releasing, praying and releasing, praying and releasing! If we continue to pray, somewhere down the line that prayer bowl will be full and God will have to release His power to our lives, because that's just the way He has it set up.

PRAYING WHEN ALL IS BLEAK

Continuing to pray when all is bleak is one of the greatest challenges that we have as Christians. Even knowing the process that must come to fulfillment, because we lack support from friends and family, our efforts many times go off-line. Because these labors are ones of faith, even Heaven itself does not offer much encouragement to help us along the way. We are pretty much left to ourselves, on our own, as far as our feelings are concerned. It is with that in mind I close this chapter, going back to the Scripture in Ephesians that we started with. When we begin to analyze words like *exceeding, abundantly,* and adjectives similar to them, many times it's hard to picture in our minds what they really mean. I know that we can go to the dictionary and they will give us definitions that will partly help us understand. Nevertheless, we really don't have a complete comprehension and therefore feel left out in the dark.

I would like to take the time now to personally share with you what Ephesians 3:20 means to me. In the aftermath of my evil day (see my first book, **An Evil Day**), there was not much in life that I was left with. The losses that I incurred were not only great in number, but also in emotional damage. The material losses could, in time, be replaced, although owning a home in California was extremely difficult. It was the emotional and spiritual injuries that had my concern. I was forced into starting life all over again beyond the age of 50. It is usually at this time of life that one is looking to plan his retirement, not returning to the job force at square one.

It was somewhat iffy to secure a ministerial license and I knew that I could not depend on my bachelor's degree in accounting because I had not used it in over 20 years. How was I going to provide for my family, much less find a new wife under these conditions? I had been so drained emotionally that not only did my physical body begin to break down, spiritually I just was not the same. If God were to perform the miraculous, it would have to be a sovereign move because I just didn't have anything left to add. This is the sad condition where *"he that is able to do exceeding abundantly above all that we ask or think"* found me.

The only thing that I had going for me at that time was that for some reason, I continued to pray. Despondent as I was, I continued to pray. For every loss that I incurred, for every pain endured, I continued to pray. For every tear that was shed, for every time my heart felt like breaking, I continued to pray. Little did I know that the prayer bowl in Heaven was filling up and when it did, what I received from above was truly more than I could have asked or thought.

The process was deliberate, but it began in the repairing of my mind and heart. Slowly I began to think clearly and emotionally I was becoming stable. I noticed the change when I found myself laughing again, something that I had not done in a long time. The healing process continued when I met the most wonderful woman in the world, my future wife, Maria. One day I had sat down with the Lord and I jotted down 12 attributes that were essential in the woman I would call my next wife. Talk about a wish list, but because it was important to me, it became important to Him. I found in her everything that I ever wanted and more (she's good-looking, too, an added bonus). Her ability to make me laugh has had such a great impact on me that I find myself with so much more vigor and zest for life. This in effect has influenced my ministry to the point that my anointing now is more powerful than it has ever been (see Chapter 7).

It all came about because I continued to pray. Don't ever let the enemy convince you that your prayers do not count. There is one last Scripture I would like to leave with you to assure you that they do.

> *You number my wanderings; put my tears into Your bottle; are they not in Your book?*
> (Ps 56:8)

While the prayers that you pray are being saved in a bowl in Heaven, God also puts every tear shed in a bottle. If our prayers are not enough of a reminder of the responsibility that He has to provide for us, then surely a bottle full of tears will do the trick. In your time of waiting, when words are hard to come by, your tears will have just as much of an impact as your prayers do. Just keep on praying!

Chapter 10
BEING SET UP FOR GREATNESS

*Then he set up the pillars by the vestibule of
the temple; he set up the pillar on the right and
called its name Jachin, and he set up the pillar
on the left and called its name Boaz.*

(1 Kings 7:21)

Every time we hear the phrase, "being set up," it
always brings up negative responses. It is astounding to
think that if we take a closer look, there are more positive
definitions (26) than there are negative (2) according to
Webster's Dictionary. I will not take the time to show here
all 26 of those definitions, but I would like to mention a
few that do stand out. "Being set up" means to raise to and
place in a high position, to cause or create, to place in
power (authority), to raise from depression, to make proud.
The others follow along the same lines, yet it is the
negative definitions that seem to get stuck in our craw.
They say that "being set up," means to be put in a
compromising or dangerous position by trickery or deceit.

That is the definition that usually comes to mind when
we hear someone say that a person is being set up. In fact,

the entire phrase that we usually hear is, "being set up for a fall."

In spite of that, the Lord uses the phrase "set up" to bring our minds back to the positive. He uses it that we might concentrate on the direction that our blessings are coming from. All blessings begin in Heaven and make their way to Earth, where we His children are the beneficiaries. It is a little reminder that as children of God, He has raised and placed us in a higher position, not only in power but in authority as well. When we are set up by God, it is with the intention to take us out of our depression and make Him proud. This is what God will do for us.

> *The LORD will open to you His good treasure, the heavens, to give the rain to your land in its season, and to bless all the work of your hand. You shall lend to many nations, but you shall not borrow. And the LORD will make you the head and not the tail; you shall be above only, and not be beneath, if you heed the commandments of the LORD your God, which I command you today, and are careful to observe them.*
>
> (Deut 28:12-13)

What's the catch? We need only to heed the commandments God has given us so that the promises of greatness may come to pass. He is willing to open up the windows of Heaven to rain on our work with unrestrained favor. We will rise to the head of the class and not lag behind, because He has proclaimed it.

We will be leaders in our communities, churches, and

families, making such an enormous difference in the lives of others that all will stand up and take notice of the achievements that God has led us to. Our influence will be so great on society that they will come to us for answers, not only in the faith but in other disciplines in life as well. We have undoubtedly been set up for greatness!

A WIDOW WHO IS SET UP

There is a passage in the Old Testament where we find a widow who appears to be set up for a fall (2 Kings 4:1-7). Her life as a prophet's wife was a good one. Her husband, who had the respect of the people, permitted a life without much conflict. All of life's necessities were being taken care of by the ministry of her husband, she pretty much lacked nothing. The Scriptures go on to say that suddenly, without warning her husband died, leaving her with a mountain of unpaid bills. She had never worked a day in her life, neither was it lawful for a woman to do so. How was she supposed to handle this situation? Why would God allow such bliss for a period of time, only to have it taken away so abruptly? Had she really been set up for a fall? The more she analyzed her plight, the bleaker it got. There was no job, no money, and no way out.

It was at this time that Elisha the Prophet passed by. With somewhat of a simple question, he merely asked, "What do you have in your house?" By this time, anything of value had either been sold off or taken away by the creditors, and in her mind the Prophet was just beating a dead horse. She blurted, "A jar of oil," as if that was going to do any good. He just wanted to make sure that she was willing to give up the little bit she had in order to produce a great miracle.

The Lord continues to work in our lives in the same

manner. He continually asks us to use what we have, even if it's not good enough to produce the answer, because He knows in His wisdom that through His Spirit He can always make up the difference. He asked Moses what he had in his hand, and when he responded, "only a rod," it was enough to produce the signs and wonders that ultimately convinced Pharaoh to let the children of Israel leave Egypt. It was but a jawbone that Samson used to defeat his enemies. David had a psalm to calm an angry king, and Esther used her consecration to help Israel avoid annihilation. We can neither forget the little boy who gave up his two fish and five loaves to feed thousands and thousands of people. God will always use what is given to Him, no matter how small or insignificant. Never underestimate the power of God.

IT'S ALWAYS DOABLE

The Prophet asked of her something doable. She was to go to her neighbors and borrow as many vessels as she possibly could. It wasn't like God was asking her to go out and borrow money. The stress level of the request was about as difficult as asking a neighbor for a cup of sugar. God was using baby steps to increase her faith. The enormity of the blessing then was placed on her willingness to ask. *...you do not have because you do not ask.* (James 4:2) Logic would say to borrow as many vessels as could be filled by the one jar of oil she had in her possession. Her faith would say, "There has to be a reason why the Prophet asked me to borrow as many as I could, so I am going to go all out and see what I can get." Logic will always shortchange us in the realm of faith. God always wants to bless us above all that we can ask or think, yet we question His love for us and settle for less.

I would like to take a sidebar at this time to write something about this passage that is extremely important. As this woman wove her way through faith to produce her miracle, the greatest decision that she made in the process was that she involved her two sons. She fully understood that what was about to happen was going to increase her faith to levels that she had not yet known. Like most of us who will depend on our authority figures to do the heavy work, I'm sure she was accustomed to letting her husband handle the hard stuff. But here she was right in the middle of witnessing the greatest miracle that God had done for her personally, and her boys were there as well. She wanted to make sure that they had a bird's eye view of the hand of God moving in their lives at this time of great need. From this experience, they would never be able to deny the ability of their God and His love for them. As wonderful as all of our church programs are, I honestly believe we have taken specialization in ministry to the extreme. We separate the entire family by groups, and although many times it can be to our advantage, there's something to be said about worshiping God as a family.

The reason why I had become a lover of "prayer" is because the witness I had in seeing my mom pray, both in church and at home. When we would pray together, it was the example that she set that unleashed me to have the freedom to seek God with all my heart and soul. In the good times and the bad times, her worship never changed, and it has been the example that keeps me going in times of stress.

SHUTTING OUT THE NEGATIVE

By closing the door and shutting themselves in, the widow began to pour the oil into the empty vessels, as the

Prophet has instructed. One of the definitions used at the outset of the chapter, of "being set up," was to be placed in power and/or authority. It was this jurisdiction of authority that this woman used to generate her answer. It is usually at this juncture of understanding that we fall short. We are so power-hungry, always seeking for more, that we fail to realize if we were to use the authority God has placed in our hands, we would be far more successful in our obeying the voice of God. When the use of the widow's authority was placed in motion, it was that authority coupled with God's power that produced the greatness in her life. What was the end result? She and her children received a blessing beyond belief. Not only did she pay off all of her creditors, she had enough to live for the rest of her life. Now, let me do a little speculating here. I know the Scripture here says that she lived on what was left over for the rest of her life; however, I still don't believe it was a one-shot thing.

A onetime blessing is very similar to winning the lottery, and we all know that the Lord prefers to use other resources than the lottery to provide for us. Being financially set up for life pretty much negates the faith factor, and we know that *without faith it is impossible to please God* (Heb 11:6). I am more inclined to believe that every time the widow needed more money, that empty vessel of oil would be filled at night when all were asleep. Upon waking the next morning, the miracle would have reproduced itself and her needs would have been met once again. Can you imagine the look on the vendors' faces when she would pop in occasionally with a fresh vessel of oil? They knew she had no means of producing the oil, so where in God's name did it come from? "It came from Heaven, of course." Knowing that she was a reputable woman, it was extremely difficult refuting her claim, thus God had to get the credit for this unexplainable event. The best part of it all, God got the glory. She truly had not been set up for a fall, rather for greatness!

IT'S NOT A MISTAKE

Dreams of greatness are periodically given to those who are either too young or immature to understand their value. This was exactly what happened when Joseph woke up the one morning after having been given a dream of greatness by God (Gen. 37:5-11). He began to recount his dream to his brothers, to their dismay. Bowing down to the youngest in the family was not their idea of how a family was run. Without realizing the childishness of his boasts, he continued to ramble on about his dominion over his elders. Had he been set up for failure? No, not really, it's just God's way. I have been able to understand that God will at times give dreams of greatness to us when we cannot keep it to ourselves.

Immaturity is not a good enough reason to hold back what God would like to perform in our future. Let me explain why. God uses this opportunity to help us grow into our greatness. As we hit our bumps in the road, at times get sidetracked, even chucking it aside in disillusionment, God already knew in His foreknowledge that this was going to happen. He commences to egg us on in hopes that we will see what He sees and eventually get to the place that He promised us from the beginning.

The question is, are we willing to wait for it? In our waiting for greatness to unfold, we do not necessarily become dormant. Putting your life on pause is not what God had in mind. We are to put our best foot forward, going through whatever adversity comes our way, and waiting until God's grace kicks in. Waiting for greatness was Joseph's lifeline, because certainly his dream did not come to pass in the time frame that he had expected. As wound up as he was when he initially received his dream, he was equally agitated by the fact his dream would be placed on the back burner for several years.

To add insult to injury, it was shortly after he announced the great things God would do in his life that everything fell apart completely. He was sold into slavery because of his big mouth and sent to a far off land, forced to learn new languages and customs. He was then lied about by his boss's wife and thrown into jail. While hitting the skids in a jail cell, he began to interpret dreams for the inmates, and yet when they had the opportunity to return the favor, he was forgotten. Thirteen years had come and gone when he was asked to interpret a dream of Pharaoh's, and when successful, his life finally took a turn for the best.

MINISTERING REGARDLESS

What must be considered is the fact that while he was suffering, he was expected to minister regardless. Time and time again, I have seen several men of God resign their positions in the heat of battle. That is the worst time to let go of the fight. The Lord flourishes in impossible situations, as well should we. It is when life has taken a turn for the worst that we are refined in the furnace of affliction and consequently molded into the image of God. Dealing with Joseph's impurities and imperfections, God turned up the heat so that they could be separated from the character of God in his life. The end result was a brand-new Joseph, waiting to step into his greatness.

JACHIN AND BOAZ

It is now appropriate to discuss the Scripture that was given at the beginning of the chapter. It is indeed a hidden reminder of greatness that we find in the Old Testament. The temple built by Solomon was architecturally one of the wonders of the world at that time. The Scriptures tell us that there were two pillars set up in the porch of the temple. The king brought in Hiram, a master craftsman, from Tyre, who with skill and wisdom constructed these works of art. Among other things they were brilliantly covered with brass to purposely attract attention, shining brightly. The brass was polished so that it had a mirror-like effect, allowing passersby to see their reflections. Their beauty was only topped by their purpose. The right pillar was given the name Jachin, meaning "God will establish." The left pillar went by the name Boaz, which meant "in God there is strength." If you lapped the two meanings together they form this: God will establish you in His strength. Every morning when the priest began his stroll to the temple, just before entering he would have to pass these two pillars, reminding him that God had set him up for greatness. It did not matter what he would encounter throughout the day, there in writing he could have complete confidence that God would not only be there to help him, but to help him to great success. How does that affect our lives, seeing that it is an Old Testament passage of Scripture? God hid it just enough so that with a little bit of effort, we could find this hidden vow and partake of its magnificent blessing. The Old Testament temple is no longer around to remind us of this promise; however, it has been replaced by the New Testament temple, which the Scriptures say is our body.

Do you not know that you are the temple of God and that the Spirit of God dwells in you? If anyone defiles the temple of God, God will destroy him. For the temple of God is holy, which temple you are.

(1 Cor 3:16-17)

Today, we are the temple of God, and that same message of greatness is etched in the pillars of our hearts. In the same manner that the Old Testament temple was replaced, so has the priesthood of Levi.

But you are a chosen generation, a royal priesthood, a holy nation, His own special people, that you may proclaim the praises of Him who called you out of darkness into His marvelous light;

(1 Peter 2:9)

We as a chosen generation have taken on the royal priestly garments with all of the rights and privileges thereof. There is no reason for us to settle for second best, it is there for the taking if we want it. God will establish us in His strength and there is nothing that the devil can do to stop it.

We are our own worst enemies. Our failure to find Scriptures such as these and put them into practice only puts a limitation on the greatness that God would like to bring to our lives. In the hustle and bustle of everyday life, it is so easy to forget our place in Him and what He would like to accomplish through us. We get bogged down by the cares of life and our vision is blurred. Our storming the gates is slowed to a snail's pace because we allow the enemy to come in and steal our victory. In times like these, we must go back to the Scriptures to reinforce our position. We mustn't let pride block our way to the truth, admitting that this loss of hope happens even to the best of us, and we must all lift ourselves out of our doldrums no matter what the cost.

A TIMELY REMINDER

I had been on the road for about two weeks when I hit the wall. Those fourteen days felt like fourteen years, and I could not get home soon enough. It was a stretch where I was not in any one church more than a day. The reception that I received throughout my visit was pretty much like the weather, hot and nasty. No matter what I preached, no matter how hard I tried ministering to the individual needs of each local church, it all went unnoticed, uncared for, and unappreciated. There were times that I was in my hotel room without anyone attending to my needs. I know that it sounds like nitpicking, but the offerings were so low that I was afraid that I wasn't going to have enough money to get back home, and spending even the smallest of amounts just to eat became stressful. I began to check my life personally to see if in fact there was something I needed to do to change the climate of those churches. After seeking God sincerely, I came to the conclusion that I was just going to have to tough it out. It was after two weeks of this manner of treatment that I finally broke. Upon arriving at the last church that I was to minister to, I had already made up my mind that I was not going to minister, and whatever I could do to make this service even shorter, that would be my plan.

I remember the preliminaries being very dry, with not much movement of God's Spirit. I was mentally grinding my teeth, praying that the song service would not be over extended. Finally, when I found my place behind the pulpit and began to preach, lo and behold the response was the same as had been in the other churches.

One of the advantages of being a Pentecostal preacher comes from the fact that we receive energy from a crowd that is responding boisterously. In a church that is quieter in nature, we have to work a little bit harder to get them to respond. I neither had the will nor the strength to push them to that next level, and I really didn't care. For some reason or another, I felt convicted to ask if there were any sick or afflicted people in the congregation, and much to my dismay, a few folk stood up. I hurriedly prayed for them until I encountered a situation that I was not prepared for.

A woman had waited patiently for me to finish with everyone else when she approached the altar, walking gingerly with a cane. She was trembling noticeably and my lackadaisical spirit began an about-face. I quizzically asked what her problem was, and she said that she suffered both from arthritis and Parkinson's disease. My mind was in such a haze that I had forgotten what Parkinson's was, as she explained to me that she really did not have much control of the limbs in her body that did the shaking. She went on to say that the doctors had no hope for her in recovering, and she would just have to live with her condition. It was at that moment that a holy anger fell upon me and I became very emotional. The tears began to well up in my eyes and I could sense the Spirit of God and a special anointing begin to flow through me. He then whispered in my ear, saying something I will never forget. He said, "This is why I have called you, to bring hope to the hopeless. Now quit feeling sorry for yourself and lay hands on her that I might heal her in the name of Jesus." As I did so, there was an immediate change in her countenance. She dropped the cane, stopped trembling, and told me that the pain in her body was completely gone. I asked her if she'd be willing to take a walk for me, and with the help of the Pastor's wife she went up the aisle and back with no problem. By this time, the tears were falling uncontrollably down my face and I could not help but plead for forgiveness to a God who is ever so accommodating to do so. I had forgotten my call to greatness, and it was God's subtle way of reminding me that His promises are irrevocable. At that moment, it did not matter to me what I had just experienced the last two weeks, what God had done that night truly made up for it. The seven-hour drive home that evening felt like a stroll in the park, and nothing could put a damper on the personal message God had delivered to me.

Because we are His children and He cares for us unconditionally, we all have promises of greatness. Great or small, male or female, black or white, studied or not, we all have the same shot at greatness. Whether we get there or not has truly been placed in our hands. The buck stops here because the ball has been placed in our court. God wants us to be willing participants in His provision, and if we realize that He always has our back, we too will step into greatness.

Books Available in English

Libros Disponibles En Español

George Pantages Ministries

George Pantages
Cell 512 785-6324
geopanjr@yahoo.com
Georgepantages.com